W9-AOG-285

ALVAR AALTO

alvar aalto

by Frederick Gutheim

George Braziller, Inc.
NEW YORK, 1960

CONTENTS

ALVAR AALTO

Bᴇᴛᴡᴇᴇɴ ᴛʜᴇ two wars the world was given a new architecture. Its revolutionary temper was marked by a sober, analytical functionalism; and by a crusading fervor. The German architect, Walter Gropius, who founded the celebrated design school called the Bauhaus in Dessau, remains the best exponent of sober functionalism. The French architect, Le Corbusier, a prolific author of hortatory tracts on modern design, filled the missionary role. While both architects have since moved on to a more flexible and personal style, their work of the period 1920–1940 seems shrill and brittle in retrospect. It lacked too many of the qualities of great architecture to be wholly satisfying. Alas, for all its preoccupation with social purpose and human use, it lacked humanism. For all its keen intelligence and scientific basis, it lacked wit. And for all its analytical and historical rationality, it lacked art.

Interest in the work of Alvar Aalto, who became increasingly well known as an international architect during the decade of the 1930's, grew to a pitch of enthusiasm as it was recognized that he embodied just those qualities of humanism, wit and art our revolutionary architecture had lacked. Out of the remote north, just 30 years old when he won the competition for the design of the great sanatorium in Paimio in 1928, Aalto was an appealing figure.

Aalto's youth and romanticism were certainly more piquant to Europeans and Americans because of his origin in remote Finland. (He played on it, on Finnish *sisu* [fortitude], winter sports, steam baths and the rest, like Maurice Chevalier and his French accent.) But these characteristics found expression in a highly original series of designs, not limited to architecture but extending to the design of furniture, glass, textiles; and to the most comprehensive conceptions for housing, city and regional planning. It was, indeed, in the field of exhibition design—with its unique demand for a total design to create a theatrical world of illusion—that Aalto received his first and most decisive opportunities.

To a world apprehensive that industrialization, standardization and mass production meant that individual artistic expression and indigenous regional characteristics would be extinguished, Aalto brought a heartening reassurance that stemmed both from his intensely vital personality and his role as the exponent of a profound architectural tradition of Scandinavia and the Baltic states. In the quarter century since, other architects have further relieved these earlier anxieties. Indeed, the entire development of today's architecture under the impact of a new structural expressionism, has steadily

9

emphasized the individuality of buildings and their designers, to say nothing of more plastic, sculptural building forms themselves. But if we were to name the great architects in whose work these characteristics first appeared, other than Aalto there would be only the now departed Frank Lloyd Wright.

1. THE SEARCH FOR A NATIONAL ARCHITECTURE

THE NATIONAL independence of Finland, declared December 6, 1917, during the chaos of the Russian revolution, climaxed an awareness of linguistic and cultural identity that had been growing since 1835. For many centuries a part of the Swedish political realm, Finland had been an autonomous part of the Russian empire since the early nineteenth century. In internal affairs its autonomy was complete, and the western legislation (the code of 1734) remained in force. At the time national independence was achieved, Finland's orientation was definitely toward western Europe, its sense of national individuality was highly developed, and the industrial revolution had so altered matters in the production of cellulose and in transportation that the new nation was committed to a strong position in world trade.

These considerations both reflected and emphasized Finland's geographical position as a border country. Not only did it stand between Scandinavia and Russia, but the Gulf of Finland was for long the practical northern fringe of Europe; and the most thickly populated part of the country stood as a boundary between the world trade routes to the south and a relatively unexplored and extensive hinterland reaching north to the Arctic Ocean. In the economic development of Finland, not only the rich timber resources but extensive water power and minerals in the northern districts have become important factors in recent years. It is today, to employ an example of some architectural significance, the largest producer of copper in Europe.

Alvar Aalto, born in central Finland in 1898, was studying architecture in the Technical College in Helsinki during the revolution of 1917. He still enjoys the recollection of the Russian grand dukes, who had fled to the relative stability of Helsinki, and had gathered in the leading hotel, the Seurahuone, (which had been designed by Aalto's professor, Lindegren) under fire from Russian sailors in the station plaza. In his youth the great buildings all dealt necessarily with the cultural imperative: the search for a national architecture. This was the aspiration of Siren's parliament building, of Lindegren's Olympic stadium, and—perhaps most of all—Eliel Saarinen's railroad station in Helsinki, conceived as the meeting point between the eastern and western worlds.

When Aalto commenced his first group of important architectural commissions for exhibition pavilions, he found they, too, posed sharply the problem of national architecture. His first independent architectural work was the design of an industrial exhibition in Tampere in 1922 (plate 1). At about the same time he was engaged as a staff architect on the design of the 1923 Gothenburg exhibition. This led to his association with the architect Erik Bryggman in the design of the exhibition celebrating the 700th anniversary of the city of Turku in 1929 (plate 2).

This was the background to Aalto's first great international success, the indigenous yet international Finnish pavilion in the 1937 Paris international exposition. A poem of wood, the pavilion used a structure of poles bound together with withes to form columns (plate 6), and a beautifully detailed board-and-batten wall (plate 7). Within these undulating walls an atrium provided natural lighting for exhibits (plate 8). To a world audience, oppressed by the strident and prophetic competition expressed in the Nazi and Soviet pavilions, the appeal of serenity, naturalness and sensitivity in Finland's pavilion was irresistible.

The theme of the undulating wall had been explored in the ceiling of the library at Viipuri. But beyond its assertive irrationality (in architecture the equivalent of Miro and Arp) and visual excitement, its denial of the rule of geometry and its affirmation of the organic nature of structure became a symbol of political freedom. To this theme Aalto returned with even greater originality and authority in the Finnish exhibition in the New York World's Fair of 1939. While limited to the rectangular space offered in a group of exhibition halls provided by the fair, Aalto's interior took a strongly architectural form (plates 41, 42). Despite these limitations, the result has been recognized as "the most daring piece of architecture" in a fair which included such memorable buildings as Markelius' Swedish and Niemeyer's Brazilian pavilions.*

Other exhibition buildings with a similar character were built for the 1937 agricultural fair at Lapua in northern Finland. Here a willingness to adapt a sophisticated design to relatively elementary construction methods yielded a building of rugged strength. In 1946 he created an exhibition building at Hedemora. A decade later in 1956 he designed Finland's pavilion in the Venice Biennial. But in these there is neither the historical imperative, nor the imaginative genius of the decade of the 1930's. Finland's superb building in the Brussels exposition in 1958, was the work of a much younger architect, Reima Pietila, who—like Viljo Rewell—is one of those architectural meteors that occasionally flash across the northern skies.

Through his accomplishments in exhibition architecture, commissions generally won through design competitions, Aalto established his position at home and abroad as the chief vehicle of Finnish architectural expression. Saarinen's departure for the United States in 1923 had removed the only other really towering architectural figure. After that he stood alone.

2. FOUNDATION STONES

THE OPPORTUNITIES of exhibition buildings, which Aalto had been quick to grasp, were ephemeral. Beyond their limits lay the needs of a new nation for industrial plants and housing, for hospitals and libraries, for town halls and civic buildings. It was in these more enduring structures that a lasting contribution was to be made. They are chiefly recorded in the designs for the municipal library at Viipuri, a newspaper office building and printing plant at Turku, the tuberculosis sanatorium at Paimio, and a country house, the "Villa Mairea," for Mr. and Mrs. Harry Gullichson near Noormarku. All

* Siegfried Giedion, *Space, Time and Architecture*, 1949, p. 468. The historian, perhaps in belated recognition of Aalto's significance in continuing spatial developments he had earlier recognized in high baroque architecture, added an entire chapter on Aalto to this edition of his work, a modern classic of architectural history.

were located in Finland. The completion of this work occupied the decade of the 1930's, and constituted the solid foundation for Aalto's architectural renown.

The Viipuri library (plates 9–17) was won in competition. Its uncompromisingly modern design so startled the fathers of a neighboring church that a long period of delays and harassments ensued. In the seven years that elapsed before the completion of the building, Aalto's original design matured and took on a characteristic richness and originality in detail. The final building, while bold and clear in plan, was marked chiefly by its careful handling of lighting—so important both to libraries and to conditions in the long northern winters—and its shelves, panelling, furniture and other fully integrated details. The most noteworthy features of the library were its depressed, traffic-free study room; its unique, shadowless natural illumination, provided by 57 circular light wells piercing the ceiling; and its auditorium with its wave-like wood ceiling (plate 17), whose natural acoustical properties (plate 14) confer upon every member of the audience the advantages usually reserved wholly for the speaker on the platform.

The building was planned in two main blocks, one containing the library functions, the other the auditorium and a series of smaller committee and discussion rooms. The library space was subdivided by areas and levels into a control area, from which the entire library could be supervised and the movement of books regulated; a large reading room (plate 16); open stacks for study and reference; and a children's reading room. The lighting of this area was without doubt its most important characteristic As described by Simon Breines, one of the few who visited and wrote about the building before its destruction in 1940 when Viipuri and the entire province of Karelia were ceded to the Soviet Union, "A reader's book is lit from many indirect sources at once and a white page cannot reflect light up into his eyes. The books on the shelves are safe from the harmful effects of direct sunlight. The vast room is bathed in a soft, shadowless light, ideal for reading, conducive to quiet. At night the artificial light is reflected from the high white walls above the bookcases, and is equally restful and diffused." *

In contrast to the windowless portions of the building occupied by the library, the auditorium looked out through clear glass into the surrounding park. In addition to the ceiling, made (as Mr. Breines carefully points out) of 30,000 knotless strips of Karelian pine, from an entire tract of dead forest, the building announced Aalto's determination to seek decorative values in the color, grain and treatment detail of the natural wood. Stair rails, shelves, wall panels, as well as furniture provided this contrast to the generally white interior.

While one may regret the "passing" of this undisputed architectural masterpiece, Aalto has employed some of its characteristic features in later buildings, notably in the library of the Pension Bank (plate 76) and the library of the University of Jyväskylä.

The tuberculosis sanatorium at Paimio (plates 18–23), a village not far from Turku where Aalto spent much of his early professional life, was commissioned after a competition in 1928 and commenced in 1932. Its functional plan, reinforced concrete structure, its large scale and uncompromising modern design related it to the interna-

* *Alvar Aalto, Architecture and Furniture*. With essays by Simon Breines and A. Lawrence Kocher.   Museum of Modern Art, New York 1938. p. 10.

tional architecture of the day. Aalto's name was immediately joined to those of Le Corbusier and Gropius.

The sanatorium is a sun-trap. Its wings are disposed, oriented and related to each other to allow each patient to receive the morning sun on his bed. The rooms for 290 patients are in one long wing of the hospital, six stories high, facing southeast. Corridors follow the north walls, their length mitigated by natural lighting. Open-air terraces and balconies are located at the east end of each floor, oriented a bit farther to the south, with provision for both large and small groups of patients.

In a separate wing to the north, dining rooms and lounges are located, with equally careful orientation to the position of the sun at different times of the day. They constitute what Aalto calls "the hotel area." Kitchens are in an adjoining block. The two principal wings are joined by circulation and service elements. Other hospital requirements, including doctors' (plate 23) and nurses' quarters and utilities are provided in separate buildings.

Clearly the basic idea of the hospital, around which everything else revolves, is the daily routine of the patient in his hospital room. The design of the room itself is executed with the utmost care (plate 22). Each unit serves two patients. Special window details insure ventilation without drafts. Panel heating is delivered from ceilings. Wardrobes of plywood are hung from the walls. Hand basins designed to be splash proof are hung on the corridor wall. Opposite, a continuous working table runs under the windows. All other illumination in the room is in back of the patient. Walls are painted a soft, neutral tone, with the ceiling somewhat darker—a restful effect when one is lying in bed. Finally, the acoustical treatment of the corridor wall deadens the usual hospital noises.

In its programmatic detail, the influence of the Paimio hospital has been enormous. Unfortunately, its humanistic philosophy has been less emulated than its functional expression. The subsequent examples that have reached the high plane of Ganster and Pereira's Lake County (Illinois) Tuberculosis Sanatorium have been rare. Even in Finland such a hospital as Jonas Cedarcreutz's splendid Regional Hospital of Middle Finland at Jyväskylä is the exception. The reason is clear: it is the fully-integrated perfection of the Paimio hospital as a whole, not its ingenious details, that make it the important building it still is.

In 1929, the year following the start of the sanatorium, Aalto was commissioned to design the newspaper offices, printing plant, together with additional offices and a separate apartment unit, for the Turku newspaper, Turun-Sanomat (plates 24–25). The site faces a conventionally restricted urban street (plate 24) and the result is probably the most extremely rationalized building of Aalto's career—more so even than his subsequent industrial structures. The reinforced concrete building presents a white facade marked chiefly by steel window sash in long strips, plate glass display windows, and geometrical regularity. The interior corridors and offices are small in scale but reflect contemporary German standards. The most attractive and memorable element of the building is the deep basement press room, where the reinforced concrete pylons are exposed and lit to make full use of their expressive value (plate 25). Their sculptured shape antedates by a decade those Le Corbusier was to use in his Marseilles apartment house.

Standing in Turku, hard by the principal works of Aalto's contemporary, Erik Bryggman, one is forcibly reminded that to most of Finland Aalto appears as the disciple of the new rationalism. It is Bryggman who seems to them the romantic, the nature-loving humanist—and, indeed, there is his Burial Chapel to show it. But its non-structural prettiness shows, too, Finland's need for the discipline and humanistic order which Aalto provided. These qualities found an extreme expression in the Turun-Sanomat building, but they are presented without apology in the Paimio Sanatorium and the Viipuri Library.

Entering the decade of the 1930's, Aalto's work included a railroad station in Tampere and an art museum in Reval, Estonia, neither of particular significance. At the end of the decade, however, he produced two buildings which may well be considered together because they involve that remarkable woman, client and executive, Mairea Gullichson who created the famous Artek enterprise, and whose husband was Harry Gullichson, chairman of the board of the Ahlstrom corporation, until his death in 1955. Much of Aalto's career was associated with these two powerful individuals.

With Mrs. Gullichson, Aalto designed in 1937 the Savoy restaurant (plate 5), located on the top floor of a new office building in Helsinki, with a terrace overlooking the Esplanade. The interior was the most perfect realization of integral architecture. Aalto's furniture had just come into mass production (plates 43–45) and was used to complete the superb interior of a most agreeable and excellent restaurant, further endowed with that accessory rare in the north, a dining terrace overlooking a park. It is a pleasure to report that this restaurant is perfectly maintained today and is, in fact, the best and most publicly accessible example of Aalto's mature style of the pre-war years.

His country house for the Gullichsons stands on family lands near Noormarku, about a hundred miles northwest of Helsinki. Here one finds a unique monument to Finland's industrial and social development—three villas, each built a third of a century apart, each perfect of its day, and each faithfully preserved and maintained in the style of the period. In the adjoining estate is found the early sawmills and iron works, the mill ponds and other features of the early industrial landscape. This is the monument to the Ahlstrom family, founders of Finland's outstanding horizontal trust, which today owns mines and standing timber, water power and shipyards, glass and plywood concerns, cellulose and paper factories, plastics and chemicals firms—all of them developed from the timber resources which Antti Ahlstrom as a poor young man began to assemble in the mid-nineteenth century. At Noormarku stands the 'Gothick' wood chalet he built in 1872—the veritable house of a lumber magnate, which would be equally at home in Maine, Minnesota or the state of Washington. A few hundred yards away is the house built by his son, Walter Ahlstrom, a large and handsome wood frame mansion with white plaster walls, Dutch ornamental detail, and luxuriously detailed interiors. The third house of this group is the "Villa Mairea," built by Walter Ahlstrom's daughter, Mairea Gullichson. She insisted, with plain logic, that she have her own house of her own period and taste, just as her father and grandfather had.

What Aalto created was a house fully as important as those three other great contemporary masterpieces: Wright's Falling Water, Le Corbusier's Villa Savoye, or Mies' Tugendhat House (the last, alas, destroyed). In every sense it must be regarded as a collaboration with an exceptional client. In Mairea Gullichson are transplanted those executive abilities so evident in her father and grandfather. Determined to follow a life of art, she studied painting in Paris, and travelled widely in Europe and the Mediterranean. Her great accomplishment, however, lay in the creation of the Artek Company, best known for its manufacture and world-wide distribution of Aalto's birch plywood furniture, but equally a unique cultural force in Finland through its exhibitions of painting and its introduction of the world's best examples of industrial design.

The Villa Mairea (plates 26–32) is not a dwelling so much as a large vacation house, a retreat where one can paint or write, a place to entertain one's friends, or simply a sheltered place to relax. Its charm reflects its success in creating a stimulating and appropriate framework for these moods and activities. The house is carefully zoned into living and service areas, and in this lies much of its wonderful sense of privacy. Although the living areas are a single continuous open space, the dining area is visually separate. The large living room (plate 32) is further subdivided into a relatively secluded area surrounding the traditional raised Finnish hearth, and a large, well-planted solarium with huge windows. Within the L-shaped plan, connected by a loggia oriented for sun-bathing, is the Finnish steam bath in a separate building and the plunge—a small, informally curved, swimming pool (added in 1946, following the revival of enthusiasm for the *sauna*) (plate 31). The house stands in a clearing hewn in the dense forest of fir, and one looks directly from it into the rough bark columns and the tall undergrowth of the forest floor.

The house displays most of Aalto's famous details of this period: the slatted wood ceiling, the columns bound by willow withes, exterior venetian blinds, exposed vertical board and batten, poles used as space dividers, ornamental staircases of daring structural ingenuity,* the counterpoint of intensely natural and highly industrialized building materials. In the hands of other architects they became clichés, but in the Villa Mairea these survive today in their original freshness and power.

It is not to such details that the house owes its architectural strength but to its clear, open plan, and its free but carefully defined flow of space. For all its lack of partitions, this is controlled and disciplined space.

In these four buildings Aalto's genius was announced to the world.

3. FACTORIES AND HOUSING

BEFORE FINLAND could have its libraries and hospitals, its newspaper plants and villas, the new nation had to create the industrial structure which, from limited natural resources, could produce the nation's wealth. The design of buildings for industry, and for the housing of their labor force, often in isolated towns, was a major part of Alvar Aalto's practice in the 1930's and again in the period of national adjustment and reconstruction following the Second World War.

The continuity of such architecture across two decades is best illustrated in the Sunila sulphate mill near the major seaport of Kotka on the Gulf of Finland. Here the wood collected over a huge area of northeastern Finland, and floated through the extensive system of lakes and canals, is delivered to a highly integrated industrial operation.

* Auguste Perret once commented, "Stairs are a measure of civilization."

From storage yards and ponds it is conveyed to the top of the plant and delivered by gravity to chopping, cooking and processing facilities. In the end the product—cellulose sheets—is delivered to ocean-going freighters moored beside the plant warehouse. Finland's industry can be put in a single word—cellulose. It is a dirty business, polluting both Finland's beautiful lakes and skies. Aalto's first industrial plant in 1930 was the sulphate pulp mill of Toppila (plate 3), where he displayed an initial mastery of the architectonic forms of industrial smoke stacks, ventilators, conveyors, processing, warehousing and transportation elements. In his hands they became as characteristic and as eloquent as grain elevators or blast furnaces. Work at Sunila was commenced in 1936 and continued until 1939. A second period of construction activity commenced in 1951 and ran until 1954. In both periods Aalto designed the major industrial structures and the supporting housing for employees and executives. The general plan (plate 34) is strongly influenced by the shelving granite which separates naturally the many small groups of houses of different types standing in the ubiquitous pines. The plant itself is carefully poised over the uncut granite of an offshore island (plate 36). The intervening blue-stained waters accomodate both stored timber and Sunila's fleet of pleasure craft.

The very first buildings at Sunila announce the determination to build a community of houses around a center with its communal steam bath and laundry. This is the neighborhood cell which has been multiplied over the years, and reinforced by larger civic and commercial centers, the most recent of which is focused on the main coastal highway. There is housing of all sorts (plates 39, 40): cottages, single-story row houses, short rows of three story walk-ups and terrace flats. Their site planning is ingenious, and the natural divisions of the site—the granite and the visual barrier of the forest—preclude any overwhelming scale. Yet Aalto's own philosophy of housing—however objective (Sachlichkeit), at this period—would not allow in any case the unlimited multiplication of a single type. ("Five hundred houses of the same sort is the absolute limit," he audaciously advised the Federal Housing administrator when he first visited the United States in 1938.) He concentrated at Sunila on making each community complete in itself, although the art has been carried to an even higher plane of diversification in the recent Finnish garden suburb of Tapiola, individual sections of which are the work of many different architects.

The industrial plant (plates 35–38) takes its form from the extreme horizontal length of the warehouse and piers, and the great height reached by the stacks. Aalto has made the most of these, as well as of the dramatic contrasting white diagonals of the conveyors. He has also given character to the establishment in its detail. The contrast of the native granite shelf and the man-made structure is pointed up by a wall of rough-hewn granite blocks encountered at the entrance to the executive offices—a native wall terminating in a superbly finished industrial structure. The vista of woods and islands in the Gulf of Finland is unexpectedly blocked by a neatly-realized, reinforced-concrete, bowstring truss. These contrasts are seldom accidental. Through them Aalto is constantly recalling the health-giving strength and continuity of that nature in which Finland is still so rich, juxtaposed with the conditions and forms of modern engineering and industry. These are lessons to which Finland's more careful observers, the Soviet engineers and industrialists, preoccupied with technical to the exclusion of human factors, are still blind; but so, too, are many here in the United States, unable to recognize in the cooperative movement, the labor union, the neighborhood association or even in the political party that strength which no individual alone can realize.

There are few other industrial projects to compare with Sunila in scale, continuity over the years, or functional diversity. Indeed, much of Aalto's industrial building is of relatively little design interest, and has not even been published. In 1930–31 he designed the sulphate pulp mill at Toppila which anticipated some of the later industrial elements in Sunila. In 1938 a paper factory at Anjala was designed. In 1945 he designed a sawmill at Varkaus, with bold vertical ribbing, and a cornice emphasizing its undulating walls. In 1949 he designed a warehouse for glass products at Karhula, and subsequently a major addition for offices and an apprentice school. Other industrial buildings, mainly at the Ahlstrom works at Karhula and Kauttua, were products of the reconstruction period.

While such isolated industrial structures continued to be drawn in Aalto's office, his attention became more engaged by the post-war industrial development of northern Finland and the need for comprehensive planning of these new works. It was not the architectural envelope for the manufacturing process alone, but the total urban environment, and the more complex and sophisticated reconciliation of human needs with technological requirements that he found challenging to the architect. In the large scale projects that came from Aalto's office, comprehensive plans for Rovaniemi, Nynäshamnin, Otaniemi, Oulu and Imatra—all of them industrial towns for the newly organized post-war economy of Finland—were far more than mere master plans for industry. Similarly, the projects for the Technical Institute at Otaniemi, the Technical College at Oulu, or the University at Jyväskylä grew from earlier undertakings of a related sort in these cities, and reflected the philosophy of comprehensive planning which Aalto had developed for industrial enterprises but later adapted to universities and to cities.

For architects in the years immediately preceding the Second World War, a prime challenge of industrialization was its application to housing. The rationalization of the production of low-cost housing had, in Germany, chiefly, resulted in the large-scale housing community. In the United States housing technology was best expressed in job organization and in the prefabricated house. When examined in the light of its historical period, it is clear that, while Aalto was aware of what was happening elsewhere, and accepted the idea of housing as an instrument of social policy, his instinctive reaction was against bigness, against regimentation and toward designs that recognized and strengthened the individual, the family and the organic community.

This essential humanism, enunciated first at Sunila, Aalto rapidly developed into a complete philosophy of housing in 1941 when Finland faced the difficulties of resettling nearly one fifth of its entire population as the result of the terms of the peace with Russia, and when it was already abundantly clear that the devastation of the Second World War would present tasks of rebuilding that dwarfed the aftermath of earlier wars. To Finland the cession of the entire rich and populous province of Karelia to the Soviet Union posed a crash problem of relocating the entire evacuated population. The evacuees were sent to towns, to farms, wherever jobs could be found or farms made, in a country where more than 70 percent of the land is covered by forest. A capital levy upon the rest of the nation financed the purchase of land and the construction of new houses. But the actual fabrication of so many dwellings in a short time strained every resource.

Aalto had seen the consequences of other "housing booms" and he dreaded the waste of tearing down and rebuilding hastily improvised shelters, standing in badly planned communities. He cited "klondikes" the world had known to illustrate how the initial barracks are replaced by minimal family dwellings which, in turn, have to be replaced because they cannot support a higher standard of living. Instead he proposed "the growing house," capable of further enlargement or development without the wasteful destruction of what had earlier been built. This essentially biological conception proposed making full use of prefabrication and advanced construction methods. Of the program initially proposed, Aalto considered that two thirds of the single units would be prefabricated, another sixth assembled by unskilled workers from factory-made standard units, and only the remaining sixth built by local craftsmen. But the architect carefully specified, "Standardization here does not mean a formal one with all houses built alike. Standardization will be used mainly as a method of producing a flexible system by which the single house can be made adjustable for families of different sizes, various topographical locations, different exposures, views etc." He prepared a detailed proposal for an experimental town of some 200 houses, illustrating it not only with production plans but with a schematic town plan. It showed, distributed around a strong community and educational core, the initial experimental settlement in dwellings of different types, and the provisions by which, over a period of time, the community would grow to occupy more extensive housing situated in other parts of the town on sites provided for at the beginning. The proposal was prophetic of much that was to come in the postwar years.

4. POST-WAR PLANNING AND RECONSTRUCTION

FROM THE FIRST arrival at Turku, passing through islands that have been called "a museum of granites," the visitor to Finland is insistantly aware of its geological framework. This intimate and detailed landscape of eskars and moraines, of granite ridges and glacial lakes, presents itself immediately to the architect as an inescapable challenge. It is the same almost everywhere in southern Finland. Coupled with the low angle of the winter sun, it presents specific conditions that are translated into architectural imperatives. It is not surprising that nearly all site planning is done over utilities drawings. At Sunila, the granite ridges compartment the housing areas into many small settlements. The north side of the conical hills that are commonplace features of southern Finland are considered unfit for human habitation because the sun seldom reaches there. These conditions breed an attitude of acceptance. One bows to nature. One learns to live with nature. And one learns to respect nature. Aalto's management of the huge masses of industrial structures, hovering over the native granite of the island at Sunila, is a case in point. The attitude is universal. Once I heard two Finnish architects discussing in scandalized tones how the foundations designed for a house had required blasting.

In the comprehensive plan for Rovaniemi, often called the "capital of Lapland,"

SCHEMATIC PLAN FOR AN EXPERIMENTAL TOWN. 1941 (From *Post War Reconstruction, Rehousing Research in Finland,* by Alvar Aalto)

The initial settlement of experimental houses is designated (a). The community center (b) and school with athletic field (c) serve both the initial and the ultimately developed community. Single family houses (d), small apartment houses (e), and row houses (f), constitute the additional housing to be built at the later stage of the town's development. The dark areas represent lakes; the hachured areas are woods; and the thin lines (as at e and f) represent contours—all schematized, of course, but together making up a characteristic Finnish landscape.

which is probably Aalto's first post-war plan, he applied the principles that had been worked out in the 1940 reconstruction proposal. Unfortunately, while the scheme was executed in part, it is not until now, nearly 15 years later that Aalto's original ideas are about to be illustrated by a large-scale housing project. This has been made possible by the intervention of the National Housing Foundation, builders of Finland's first garden city at Tapiola.

Aalto's approach to large-scale planning, enunciated at Sunila, and the site plan for the Kauttua housing development became both clearer and more systematic, and more sophisticated and mature, as successive projects came from his office. One of the most instructive was the competition-winning layout for the Finnish Technical Institute at Otaniemi in the suburbs of Helsinki. Here, along the marshy shores of the Gulf of Finland, a site similar to the nearby garden city of Tapiola, the facts of topography, foundation conditions and contour have been allowed to mould the entire design. What the architect has done is to clarify the relationship of man and nature, and to order that part of it which is man's.

Perhaps the best exercise in that seldom-practiced art of three-dimensional large-scale planning, of particular relevance to an America now engaged in extensive programs of urban redevelopment, was the plan for the hydro-power city of Oulu. By marine fill, the shallow but swift stream (which farther up is dammed at Aarne Ervi's vigorously engineered Phyakoski power plant) becomes a chain of shallow lakes, a waterscape framing the civic centers that are the essential features of Aalto's kind of city. Civic, sports and educational facilities here make a link joining the new town with the old. In this vivid plan, still unexecuted, one finds a perfect expression of Aalto's ability to give a number of modestly scaled buildings a bold and significant composition.

The town plan for the small industrial town of Säynätsalo, a short distance from Jyväskylä, the urban center of Middle Finland, was prepared in the reconstruction resettlement period of 1942–46, and preceded Aalto's celebrated design for the town hall there in 1950–51. In every sense Säynätsalo is a "new Town"—hewn out of the surrounding forest for its 3,000 population, its economic foundation that typical Finnish enterprise, a plywood factory. The careful classification of dwelling types and their coherent distribution follows closely Aalto's reconstruction philosophy. So, too, does the strong central core of civic, educational and sports facilities. But this is no schematic plan. Each dwelling type is assigned an area with natural features matching its requirements. Buildings are closely fitted to contour, to available sunlight, and to the superb views. What emerges is a community that is immediately apprehended as a whole, not a regimented repetition of standardized units but one marked by the diversity of housing that mirrors the social diversity of the community itself. And one of the consequences is that in this mere village of wooden cottages and simple brick public buildings there appear those two rarest of architectural achievements today: urbanity and monumentality.

A different problem was posed in the last of Aalto's planning projects of the reconstruction period—the market town of Imatra, in the extreme eastern part of Finland, where the cession of the east bank of the Vuoksi river to the Soviet Union necessitated a reconstruction of the cellulose plants in this region. Here again one faces a plan executed only in two dimensions, and awaiting further construction to realize its full potential. The consolidation of ownership of a number of industrial plants in the vicinity provided a further powerful force for unification of an area some 15 miles in length, within which are located eight separate communities each containing an industrial center, a residential community and rudimentary community facilities. Aalto's recently completed Vuoksenniska church is one of these (plates 102–113). To give coherence to this entire area, the architect has organized the new super-highways and provided an exceptionally large and richly developed civic center and market facilities. The result is a planned community scaled to the automobile, with a peculiar significance to the United States. It is not a town but more nearly what geographers call "an urban field." Each of the separate communities enjoys a carefully considered layout, making the most of topography, woods, lake and riverside locations. Here the common building unit is a quite standardized single-family wooden cottage standing on its own small lot. Two and three-story apartment houses, generally located close to village centers, provide a different type of housing.

Only the realization of the civic center at Säynätsalo allows one to conceive of the still unfulfilled significance of these plans for civic centers at Imatra, Oulu and the campus at Otaniemi. While the plans have been well detailed, and studied in model in every case, no conception of this sort carries the authority of a completed work. The mistakes made in Europe and America in the fifteen years that have passed since the war, the hasty improvised reconstruction on old sites, the pseudo-monumentality, the neglect of civic, cultural, educational and recreational needs in the unrelieved congestion of new housing—these are the slums of a tomorrow when higher living standards, greater leisure and mobility will be impossible in such cities. When that day arrives, we shall well understand what these plans of Alvar Aalto attempted to say.

5. *THE NATIONAL ARCHITECT*

WHAT DOES A nation expect of her greatest architect? This question is the key to the fifteen most productive years of Alvar Aalto's architecture, the time from the end of the unhappy war with the Soviet Union almost to the present day. From the two wars Finland lost territory, population, wealth and the gains of the two decades between the wars. From the settlement of "the winter war" of 1939–40 as we have noted, Finland lost her rich southern province of Karelia and had to face the problem of resettling a huge population. From "the following war," into which she was forced as an ally of Germany against the Soviet Union, she lost the northern region of Petsamo with its outlet to the Arctic Sea, suffered the devastation of war in her northern territory; and, in the final peace settlement in 1947, she ceded to the Soviet Union naval bases in the Gulf of Finland and incurred a heavy indemnity. But of still greater significance, the emergence of the U.S.S.R. as a far stronger imperial power and such changes as the extinction of the other Baltic states, brought a new political era.

Today, as the result of these changes, Finland—the old border country—finds herself again the cruel victim of geography. Her only significant frontier is with the U.S.S.R.; and with that nation she does forty percent of her trade. The clever manipulation of this trade by the Soviet Union has become a profoundly unsettling factor in Finnish domestic politics. With all her western sympathies, and in spite of the notable failure of the Finnish communist party to win votes in national elections, Finland finds herself politically circumscribed. Her political choice thus limited, she is steadily drifting farther and farther from the West. It is this, not the loss of territory and population, that is the continuing feature of the national post-war life, and from which derives the inflated currency, the sharply oriented and restricted foreign trade, and unstable post-war governments—all unmistakable signs of a debilitated national life.

But despite this feebleness, which shows no real sign of abating, Finland is making a gallant fight for her independence and her western heritage. Nowhere is this more evident than in the realm of culture. Architecture, and the work of Aalto especially, is deeply colored by these conditions.

The war years also caused Aalto to become a man of two countries, Finland and the United States. As an international cultural figure his recognition was comparable to Sibelius, and his diplomatic role in the United States was correspondingly large. Although in the interest of its wartime friendship with the U.S.S.R. the United States was officially to turn its back upon Finland, and summarily discharge her ambassador, the traditionally warm feeling between the people of the two countries was little affected by the swirling currents and international politics. Aalto accepted a professorship at the Massachusetts Institute of Technology where, for nearly six years, he devoted a substantial part of each year to his duties as professor of architecture. One further result of this service was his principal American building, Baker House (plates 46–49), a dormitory overlooking the Charles River on the M.I.T. campus. The building, which puzzled many champions of the "international style" when it was erected, can now be appreciated (despite the difficulties of translating), as the initial building of a series that was to mark Aalto's next decade, buildings characteristic of the Finnish national reconstruction. The undulating wall, the dark rough brick facades, the imaginative and flexible interior volumes—all were as different from the then contemporary architectural style as they were prophetic of Aalto's architecture in the coming decade.

Although heavily engaged in the construction of the Finnish pavilion in the New York World's Fair, in his exhibition at the Museum of Modern Art, in the inauguration of the American branch of the Artek Company, and in his housing studies, Aalto still maintained his life and practice in Finland. He served in the army during the war, designed housing at Karhula, and commenced the city plans for Säynätsalo, Avesta and Rovaniemi. This difficult schedule would have been impossible without Aino Marsio Aalto, whom he married in 1925, and who was his associate in every work until her death in 1949.

His first major post-war building in Finland, the town hall at Säynätsalo, completed only in 1950, marked the beginning of a decade of remarkably homogeneous design. It was a decade in which he built little outside Finland. Indeed, compared to his previous international activity, the architect's work was obscured by its location and the peculiarity of its style. Even the problems with which he was dealing, thrown up by the effort of national reconstruction, seemed strange despite the fact that much of Europe was fully engaged in its own reconstruction efforts.

The buildings of this period are marked equally by a turning away from the white-skinned buildings of the pre-war international style, the style originated by Le Corbusier, Gropius and Mies and which Aalto was really to end, and a response to the peculiar conditions of building in post-war Finland, with its lack of reinforcing steel for concrete construction and other specific building materials. Brick became of necessity the predominant material. This commonplace manner of building Aalto brought to original life and style by experiments in the actual sizes and shapes of brick, and in laying it up. These experiments, conducted over years, in cooperation with a single brick-making plant, are an excellent illustration of the resources of a relatively small plant, where the production runs are neither so long nor the outlay committed to a particular shape so great that flexibility has been lost.

It is as a symbol of the issues in these troubled times, when the nation itself is at stake, that we must see Aalto's most important buildings of the post-war period. Of the many, I shall select four: the town hall at Säynätsalo, a sermon of the fundamental institutions of democratic self-government; the Pension Bank, a monument to the nation's most celebrated achievement in the social services; the Hall of Culture, with its message and hope for cultural co-existence; and the University at Jyväskylä, a land-

AINO AALTO

mark toward the future generation and its teachers, and a proof that the geographical fact of provincialism does not of necessity lead to provinciality.

These four are the undramatic buildings of somber exterior hue (however luminous and colorful their interiors), of dark red brick and discolored copper roofs and trim, that characterize the architect's mature period. They are buildings of rugged strength; Aalto's favorite critic, Göran Schildt, has well described them as masculine. They are buildings of brilliant originality despite their superficial air of quiet. Above all, they are buildings in which breathes the spirit of the new, post-war Finland.

We have shown how the town hall at Säynätsalo had its origin in Aalto's general plan for this new town in the woods. While the setting, really the approach to the building, is yet to be completed, enough stands today to show how this building (plates 50–61), like all of Aalto's architecture, begins with an idea. It expresses the determination that these new settlers should have the vital assistance architecture can provide in establishing their democratic institutions of local government. It is of modest red brick and wood, and sits in the trees at the upper part of a rocky, rugged site. The program is quite typical of those northern town halls where one is never surprised to find restaurants, hotels, shops or other facilities provided for, rounding out the enterprise, or just helping pay the cost of it. At Säynätsalo half a dozen shops front on the principal street. Above them is a library, entered like the rest of the building from an upper-level courtyard. The principal access is a flight of granite stairs leading to the courtyard (plate 54). To

23

the left is the library, across the garden is a lodging for the custodian. To the right is the entrance to the town hall proper.

Once having reached the courtyard, the important thing is that the architectural atmosphere has changed. Indeed, it has been changing ever since the town hall was approached, and apprehended as a unified complex of related buildings. Like the Greeks, Aalto's monumentality is achieved by division rather than addition. And like the Greeks, the approach to his building is cloaked in the dynamic mystery of concealment, discovery, and rediscovery.

At the top of the granite stair you turn right and enter the town hall. To one side is the clerk's office. Straight ahead are other municipal offices, committee rooms, and space for small meetings. The scale is low. The brick-paved corridors are lit from the courtyard and walled in the town's product, a honey-colored birch plywood.

From the entrance you turn right and find yourself in a brick yard. Steps and walls of brick lead you up to a landing, you turn and climb again, and find yourself in the hall leading to the meeting room for the town council. Here brick changes abruptly to wood.

Upon entering the Council chamber (plate 59) you find yourself in a most spacious room. Although at the top floor of the building, you are not jammed up against the roof but stand in a room made even more spacious by its tilted ceiling. High above you, the ceiling is made even more mysterious by the famous construction (plate 61), and by the low level of lighting which leaves the upper part of the room satisfactorily remote in the dim distance. It is a Gothic trick.

The chamber itself is a poem in wood, a characteristic Aalto poem. Against the brick wall a humble map of the town is balanced—by a Léger painting! You feel that a balance has been struck; but the balance is cosmic.

The Council sits in a row at its bench, fortified by the symbols of its work: the ballot box and the gavel, each of special design, calling attention insistently to the tools of democracy. He who would address the audience has a narrow, confining space against the wall. The citizens themselves are offered three different kinds of seating. Those in the front row are the most comfortable, with backs and arms; those in the rear are without backs. It is a sly device to urge a limited number of spectators to collect in front, not scatter themselves throughout the hall. Should crowds demand it, additional numbers can be accommodated by opening folding doors; then more spectators can stand and attend the proceedings.

The lighting arrangements have been well refined. Natural light enlivens the brick wall at the council's end of the room, but it is fully screened from the audience. The only real natural light is admitted high to one side, but by means of rather large windows, made intentionally generous to avoid any feeling of confinement in the room itself. Through them is a view of treetops and the ever-changing Finnish skies—inspiration, not distraction.

You descend thoughtfully. Here the *res publica* has found expression in a uniquely sensitive way. Coming down you find yourself faced first with the library—the world of ideas and knowledge. Then a garden—the world of nature. And finally with the life of the village itself—the world of men. You move from a world of intensely compressed architectural sensation and symbol to one of more matter-of-fact life.

There is very little about the exterior view of the community hall of Säynätsalo that prepares you for this experience. Its principal facade shows only half a dozen shop fronts, totally subordinated to the dark-wood vertical grilles of the library (plate 56). There is little in the rising mass of the brick tower of the council chamber to suggest what is there. If asked what the most important thing about this view was, one would probably reply —trees. This is no architectural confection of structural expressionism. It is an evocation of man. His measure, his methods, his purposes, his institutions—these are the raw materials of this architecture.

Here is an architectural allegory. The movement of people, their actions, their relationships, the setting in which they execute their tasks have been intensified and given a higher meaning by the architect. Like poetry, this architecture succeeds by creating a world of its own, real but original. We are delighted by its novelty, but it never seems contrived. There is never a doubt that this is a natural, an organic world, in which everything is of a piece.

While the village hall is a wonderfully designed and carefully detailed building, it is also marked by the limited resources of a poor community. By contrast, the National Pension Bank is a luxurious and expensive monument to one of Finland's characteristic social institutions, the welfare insurance system. Thousands come from all over the world to study, to admire, to emulate this system. The institution is not an integral part of the government. This public service is a quasi-independent bank, with many of the characteristics of a private institution. It invests its own funds.

The design of the Pension Bank (plates 62–83) expresses this "public utility" character. The institution has 550 employees, nine tenths of them women, and its facilities compare closely to those found in an American insurance company. The work is highly mechanized. Batteries of punch card and computer machines occupy a key location in the building. The work is more like that of a light industry than an office building activity.

The ground floor contains as its principal feature the one activity which involves the customer—the Helsinki district office of the Pension Bank. To this office (plate 79) come Helsinki residents to make their payments, ask their questions, collect their benefits. It is an inspiring room, one for which the architect has reserved his greatest efforts, and the activity of which he has intensified, made tangible and personal in contrast to the surrounding more abstracted world of business.

Here the space is organized in a series of open cubicles of special design. Brass, black leather, and fine wood give this area a unique tone, rather like a fine ship. Above this room floats one of the world's remarkable ceilings (plates 69–71), a prismed glass structure like a greenhouse, in which natural light blends with artificial light, and falls evenly diffused to all parts of the room below.

Other parts of the building contain a variety of offices, laid out to provide self-contained space for working parties of about eight persons and their supervisors. There are also many features, including an employee cafeteria (plate 75) in a separate but connected building, looking onto a garden that divides this dining pavilion from the office building. The cafeteria contains an ingenious aluminum pan ceiling to radiate steam heat, but its principal function seems more to create an atmosphere totally different from that in which the employees spend the rest of their day. This is institutional dining where "you go out to lunch." A small executive dining room with a similar identity of architectural atmosphere is located on the top floor.

The most luxurious element is, of course, the board room (plate 77) and its auxiliary lounges, committee rooms, executive offices and reception area. The scale here is intimate, but the treatment is rich, colorful and significant. Board and committee rooms, as well as the related reception and lounge areas, are splendidly detailed, each with its own special furniture, fabrics and interior decoration, and each with its own lighting fixtures (plates 80–83).

The building has also several libraries, two of them with sunken reading rooms reminiscent of the famous library at Viipuri, that building lost to the Soviet in the war of 1941 which Aalto once sorrowfully described as "still standing but having lost its architecture." The libraries include one for recreational reading (plate 76) and one for study and language seminars. In all of them the atmosphere is perfect, the lighting steady and excellent and—most important of all—there is no through traffic.

The disposition of this complex building with its many parts and functions on a constricted urban site of awkward triangular shape (plate 63) is an instructive illustration of Aalto's method. The north side faces the apex of the triangle, its dark and perpetually shaded elevation emphasized by the bronze doors that give it the character of a security vault. By contrast the southern elevation throws open its many windows broadly to the sun and toward a vista down a long esplanade to the flashing open water beyond (plates 64, 65). By keeping his buildings low on the southern side, and locating them at the periphery of the site, Aalto has found space for courtyards and an open park that is handsomely landscaped and fitted up with a continuously flowing stream of water terminating in a fountain.

Space has been organized by subdividing the building's several elements, juxtaposing their masses and emphasizing their relationships. As at Säynätsalo, monumentality is thus achieved in the movement of people within spaces, and the careful preservation of a human scale; not by creating great crushing masses of structure.

The University (plates 84–87) lies at the edge of the provincial city of Jyväskylä in Middle Finland, and stretches out to the dense surrounding forest. It is a campus of concept familiar to the United States, but still uncommon among Europe's older urban universities. Students are provided with dormitories and eating halls as well as classrooms, assemblies, libraries and auditoriums. What Aalto is speaking about here is maturity. He has designed a college for men and women, not boys and girls. The contrast is all the more striking because half of the institution is given over to school rooms for practice teaching, and the grounds are occupied by young children as well as college students. This derives, of course, from the position of the University as a teacher's college and, indeed, it is just emerging from that more specialized status to the more comprehensive aspirations of a university.

In the newest building, containing the library and a "festival hall" as well as classrooms and administration offices, the note of sophistication is struck with the utmost clarity. In the main hall, a staircase reminiscent of the M.I.T. Senior House at once raises the design level to the most cosmopolitan (plate 89). Nothing is compromised because this is a provincial town in the back woods of central Finland. Instead it is forcibly reiterated that Jyväskylä is the intellectual center of this part of the nation, and acts accordingly.

The staircase leads on one level to the auditorium. Once again, it is divided by solid sliding walls, allowing the entire space to be used as two separate, acoustically independent halls, or thrown into a single audience. Once again the lighting fixtures are used to provide decorating interest, but more fundamentally to modify, characterize and mold the space itself. The library is Viipuri again—with a sunken reading room, totally surrounded by books and natural lighting from deep circular troughs covered with "bubbles." Larger than the similar libraries in the Pension Bank, it is the most ambitious library plan Aalto has created since the war.

The classrooms are thought of as individual rooms rather than designed uniformly to serve average purposes, with size, fenestration, equipment according to their requirements. Perhaps they will not endure forever that way, but certainly it will be no more difficult to change them into something else than to change uniform rooms for mythical "average conditions."

From this heart of the university stretch two long wings, one containing dining halls for faculty and students, and dormitories. The other wing and the open space between will be devoted mainly to sports. In this complex perhaps the most interesting structure is the university commons, an L-shaped space, the larger part of it under a boldly trussed roof which supports high windows over a solid brick wall. The opposite side looks out into a garden, made into a little courtyard by the other part of the dining hall (plate 88). Often only a few students are eating, and they are drawn to the smaller, more intimate space; but there are other times when all seats are taken. A separate faculty dining pavilion is built of granite, a "high table" itself in this academic gathering of buildings.

The Hall of Culture (plates 91–101) stands in a proletarian quarter of Helsinki, an institution created by the cultural organizations sponsored by several left-wing political parties, so left indeed that the building barely escaped having a Soviet architect. It contains a cinema—that useful and profitable adjunct, a small apartment house, and—its principal element—a concert hall with the usual lounges and services. The hall accommodates not only musical performances but the dance, and it is equipped to serve quite large conferences and assemblies. It is fully provided with broadcasting and recording equipment, and a number of seats have connections with the simultaneous translating system.

The concert hall (plates 97–101) is a straightforward, functional room given a superb flexibility to allow it to meet these varying demands. A rather high proscenium and an apron stage projecting well into the auditorium are well suited to this objective. The first dozen rows of seats are on a flat floor, and can be moved and stored in an adjoining space on the same level, thus opening the space for social purposes or meetings. Another dozen rows of seats enjoy gradually rising sight lines. Beyond these the demands of larger audiences are satisfied by the extension of one part of the house by another dozen rows with a still steeper rise which can be shut off by sliding walls if not required.

Some characteristic Aalto features to be noted here are the tilted ceiling, side walls with specially arranged (and replaceable) plywood and acoustical panels, and a splendid lighting system.

The entire house is elevated over a ground level lobby, with refreshment facilities, coat checking and lavatories. There is little effort toward decoration as such. Indeed, none. But the typical Aalto ceramic tiles line the busiest parts of the lobby (as they do in nearly all public spaces in the Pension Bank, where they have a greater variety of colors) and special lighting fixtures provide the architect's "signature."

Again, the architect here is confronted with a difficult and irregularly shaped site. He has allowed the forms of the concert hall to shape the exterior elevation of the building, and his original resolution of this shape in brick with its brooding dark copper roof is as powerful as the cathedral at Albi. The sunlight falling on the curved surfaces of the red brick wall has that quality, too rare in architecture today, of gradually changing as it passes around the surface. It is light, indeed which moulds and informs this facade.

The brick style of the post-war decade grew naturally out of the contemporary industrial designs, both for factories and for housing industrial employees. The housing at Oulu, with its alternating bands of glass windows and brick spandrels leads directly to the Engineer's Club. The difference between utilitarian and fine building is not in the basic design or structure; it is in detailing, the finish of interiors and the richness of decoration.

Nowhere in Aalto's work is this characteristic more apparent than in the design of lighting fixtures (plates 80–83). As in the experiments with brick and glass block, Aalto's original designs for lighting fixtures would have been possible only in a country where there is a factory organized to produce limited runs of a single item. It would be impossible in a situation where the architect is forced to choose between the single hand-crafted object and the mass production line that requires thousands of copies to make the tooling-up worth while. Two hundred fixtures of original design, never to be made again, are an anomaly in most industrial countries. Even in Finland they are not the rule. But Aalto has found such a manufacturer, and with him he has brought light to the dark northern latitudes, and a special joy to the interiors of his buildings. The Pension Bank owes its wonderful variety of atmosphere to the individuality of its lighting fixtures more than to any other single factor.

This group of four buildings is not the architecture of austerity. We see a careful study of brick construction, going far beyond the nominal architectural properties of the material and the bricklayer's bonds into the shapes and nature of the bricks themselves. The architect has insisted upon the special lighting requirements of each building and each part of the building, and has found there not only the fundamental opportunity to create atmosphere with light, but an opportunity to give decorative interest and originality. In other building details, in hardware and especially in furnishings, the same philosophy is combined in fresh ways with new elements. There is no "decoration."

Always Aalto is saying that mass production and standardization are good—up to a point. Beyond that they become tyranny. He has cultivated manufacturers who are geared to making 300 copies of a lamp, or 150 chairs. Sometimes they make more; sometimes the design is improved and they run it again; but more often it has served its purpose. Perhaps such production is peculiar to Finland's smaller economy, but its results must be given a value, and weighed against the costs of designing in alternate ways, either endless production, or the uniquely crafted item.

Aalto's control of the building is seemingly absolute. Nothing escapes it. And it endures (as one can perhaps see best in the 20-year old Savoy restaurant in Helsinki). This is not only total conception of architecture: it is total realization, as it is seldom experienced.

But mark well that it is not a control imposed at the expense of the building's use, or by some arbitrary esthetic rule. It is a personal interpretation of the individual characteristics of the building based on its needs, and its consistency is given by this willingness to be confronted by specific conditions (the site of the House of Culture, or the rocks of Säynätsalo) that challenge the architect. Or the necessity in post-war Finland to build with bricks because there was no reinforcing for concrete. Or the human use of a library or an auditorium that must be satisfied.

This is responsive architecture, not the architecture of arrogance.

6. AALTO TODAY

In 1955 Aalto built Studio House in the Helsinki suburb of Munkkimiemi, a short walk from his own house, erected twenty years before. To the new building he moved his professional office which had previously been maintained in his home. This I mention to explain the relatively small office maintained by the architect. In the single white drafting room of Studio House today only eight draftsmen work. There is also a "master's atelier" for Aalto's own use, where clients are received and competitions, exhibitions or other special projects executed, a room for models and samples, a tiny private drafting room, and on a lower floor a small reception room and an office for two secretaries. A courtyard in the remodelled building is terraced like a small auditorium, and here the architect receives occasional groups of visitors.

Several years after the death of Aino Aalto, the architect was married again to the architect and designer Elissa Makiniemi who is an active member of the firm. His children, a son who is a civil engineer, and a daughter, a quondam scholar now housewife and mother, have left the home. Although ceaselessly active, Aalto gives the impression today of greater calm and dignity than in his younger and more tempestuous days when he astounded the Bauhaus by lying on the floor to study the construction of a chair, when he first conquered America with his 300 word vocabulary of basic English, or when he exhorted his students at M.I.T., when they designed a window to think of it occupied by the girl they loved. He is a laurel-bedecked, 60 year-old academician. When he goes to bed at night he re-reads all the old favorites of his youth, including *Huckleberry Finn* and *Life on the Mississippi,* Strindberg, Anatole France and the Scandinavian authors who write of strong characters with robust humor. He enjoys society, outdoor life and travel. Several years ago, after building a summer house on the lake near Säynätsalo, Aalto decided they needed a boat "to go shopping." He designed one to be built by a local boat yard. It is eleven meters long and is powered by a 95 HP American marine engine, and consumes unthinkable amounts of gasoline. His best friend dryly commented, "I think this will be the last boat Aalto designs."

Yet he designed the "Finn Trader," Finland's best post-war merchant ship. And his office today is as busy as ever with projects in Finland, outstanding among which is a huge new housing community in Rovaniemi for the National Housing Foundation, builders of the Tapiola garden city near Helsinki. There are also new designs for churches, town halls and other major civic buildings.

The change that has come about in the last few years, however, is the re-emergence of Aalto as an international architect. Today no other great architect in the world has attained an international practice of such volume. It is mainly the result of winning competitions.

The Berlin Interbau of 1957 included a tall apartment house by Aalto. This led to a still taller and more daringly planned apartment house now being completed in Bremen (plate 118). In the Volkswagen capital of Wolfsburg, Germany, Aalto is building an arts center (plates 114–117). In Sweden he won the 1955 competition for the Gothenberg town hall, and the following year another competition for the design of a marine terminal in the same city. One of his greatest designs, that for a chapel and crematorium just outside Copenhagen, was a winning competition design of 1953 and now seems to be moving ahead. In 1958 another Danish project, that for an art center at Aalborg, was commenced (plate 122). Farther afield, a large house for the Paris art dealer, Louis Carré, is under construction at Bazoches, near Chartres (plates 119–121). Finally, Aalto is the architect for the new art museum projected in Bagdad.

It is difficult to characterize these buildings, few of which have yet been completed. Perhaps the major impression is that they are emancipated from the limitations of the Finnish building economy. Yet one is conscious of continuity in purpose and in plan with the major buildings of the last decade rather than of any drastic break with it.

The fertility of imaginative conception that is marked in the interior architectural volumes has been heralded in earlier buildings. We have seen it in the ceiling of the Viipuri library, the undulating wall of Baker House, the flexible spaces of the Vuoksenniska church and the Hall of Culture. In such buildings as the projected Aalborg art center, the Wolfsburg Kulturcentrum, or the house for Louis Carré these themes, now liberated from their practical restraints, have achieved orchestral expression. They announce a new period in Aalto's work.

The Bagdad museum, to take one example, is chiefly influenced by climate. The entire structure is shaded by a roof garden used for the display of sculpture and as a terrace cafe. Its double concrete walls, responding to a study of the thick masonry walls of old local buildings, contain an insulating air space which also accommodates utilities lines. The cooling effect of the constant subsurface temperature is employed to limit the load on the museum's air conditioning system. The walls are screened from the sun by vertical louvres. These details by no means handicap Aalto's brilliant resolution of the problem of the principal gallery itself, a space 150 x 180 feet, freely cut out of the main floor of the museum. The result is the familiar Aalto combination of regularity and original architectural forms, practical nature and artistic whim, the rational business of building with the soaring architectural inspiration.

The qualities to be observed in Aalto's work over one third of a century are not ephemeral. They continue to characterize his work. They derive from firmly held convictions and they are not likely to change. How can they be summarized?

Aalto's style is architectural counterpoint. He balances the old and the new, he contrasts the natural and the technological, he alternates large expanses of smooth glass or wall with slender columns, he interrupts the routine rhythms of structure with a sculptured pier, he adds to a perfectly regular structural form another of undulating curves, or fan shape, and he juxtaposes with his buildings the surrounding nature and the movements and activity of people.

A second characteristic is continuity. Although receptive to the fresh ideas of Le Corbusier and the Bauhaus, Aalto never had to revolt against his predecessors in Finland. Indeed, like Gunnar Asplund, his first buildings show a respect for the *Jugendstil,* particularly as represented by the Finnish exponent Lars Sonck.

The characteristics of respect for the past and a modesty in appraising one's own works have also made Aalto a good teacher, and a figure which many younger architects have found it easy to admire and to emulate. In him they have found not a style to copy, but a new freedom that releases and challenges whatever creative energies they possess.

In Aalto we see the regional expression that does not deny the universality of art. His indigenous characteristics are never provincial. In his work there are echoes of peasant building, but it is never idiomatic. Rather, as a composer may commence with a few bars of a folk tune, the architectural music Aalto has invented soars beyond anything which folk culture has realized—or to which it may even aspire.

Aalto recognizes the civilizing effect of architecture. In his hands it intensifies one's appreciation both of human activities and relationships, and enhances the forms, volumes and textures of the architectural spaces themselves. He is not indifferent to the dramatic qualities of sheer structure, but when they appear in his work they are employed for purposes other than to excite. Crowded by the limitations under which he has been forced to work, Aalto has extracted the utmost from what might be called the essentials of architecture—from space, light, materials. Hard-headed and practical as his work has been, it is never mere functionalism. In his buildings there is emotion beyond sentimentality, and humor beyond whimsy. His appreciation of nature begins with man and in the end returns to man. It is not an exploitation of the picturesque or the romantic. With him, as with every great architect, buildings must be conceived as total artistic expressions. It is this which has animated his efforts (and they have been far more successful than those of any contemporary) in the design of furniture, hardware, lighting and other parts of his integral architecture. He has recognized in architecture a social obligation, and he has played upon it as upon a vast instrument to echo and to raise to still higher expression the demands of his nation, of the rising industrial classes, and of man with his unbounded intellect and imagination.

1. Industrial Exhibition, Tampere, 1922.

2. 700th Anniversary Exhibition (with Erik Bryggman), Turku, 1929. General view.

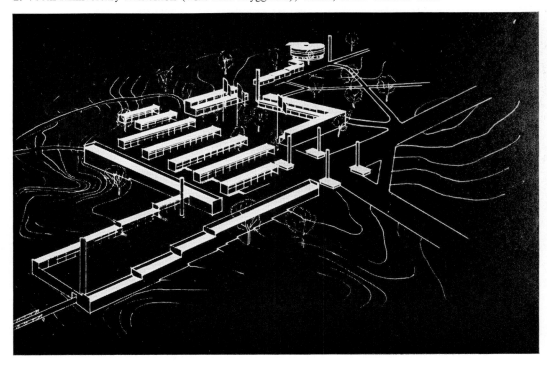

3. Sulphate Paper Mill, Toppila, 1930–31.

4. Finnish Theatre, Turku, 1927–28. Auditorium seen from stage.

5. Savoy Restaurant, Helsinki, 1937. Interior.

6. Finnish Pavilion, Paris Exposition, 1937. Terrace.

7. Finnish Pavilion. Exterior detail.

8. Finnish Pavilion. Gallery surrounding central court.

9. Municipal Library, Viipuri, 1927–35. Air view.

10. Municipal Library. Plans of first floor (above) and upper ground floor (below).

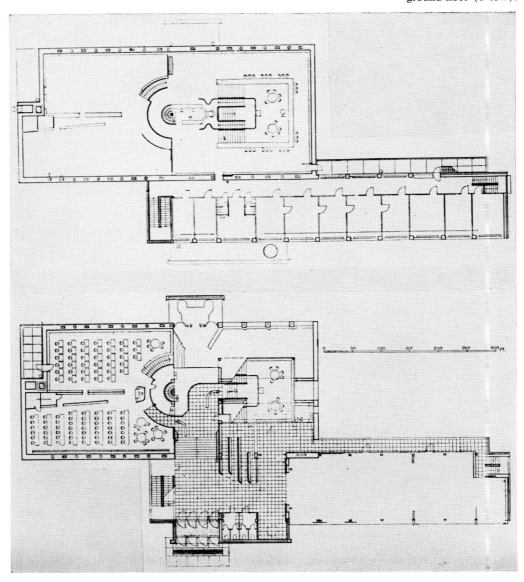

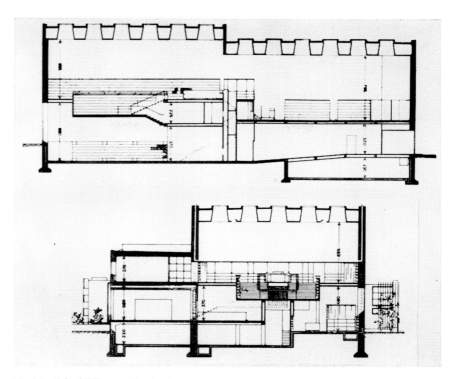

11. Municipal Library. Sections.

12. Municipal Library. Exterior detail.

13. Municipal Library. Lecture room.

14. Municipal Library. Acoustic diagram of lecture room.

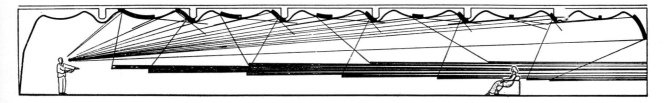

15. Municipal Library. Interior, view from lectern.

16. Municipal Library. Reading room.

17. Municipal Library. Lecture room, detail of ceiling.

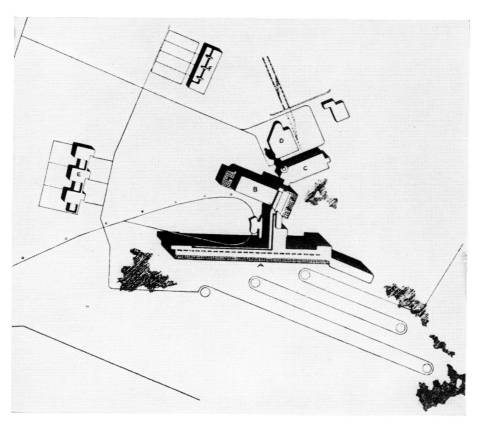

18. Tuberculosis Sanatorium. Ground plan.

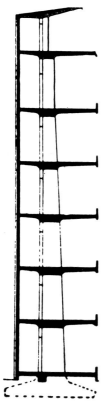

19. Tuberculosis Sanatorium. Plans.

20. Tuberculosis Sanatorium, Paimio, 1929–33.
Exterior (opposite page).

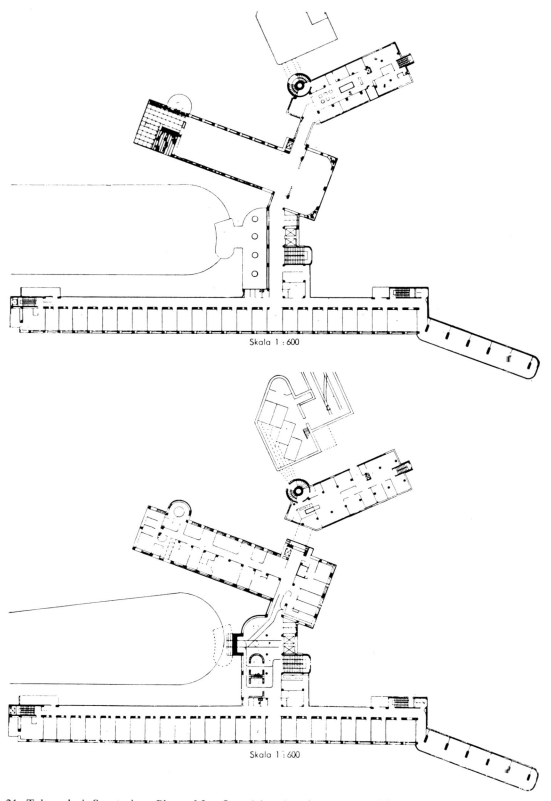

Skala 1 : 600

Skala 1 : 600

21. Tuberculosis Sanatorium. Plans of first floor (above) and upper ground floor (below).

22. Tuberculosis Sanatorium. Patient's room.

23. Tuberculosis Sanatorium. Doctors' houses.

24. Turun-Sanomat Newspaper Office, Turku, 1929–30. General view of street front.

25. Turun-Sanomat Newspaper Office. Press room.

26. Villa Mairea. Garden gate.

27. Villa Mairea, Noormarku, 1938–39. Plans of first floor (left) and second floor (right).

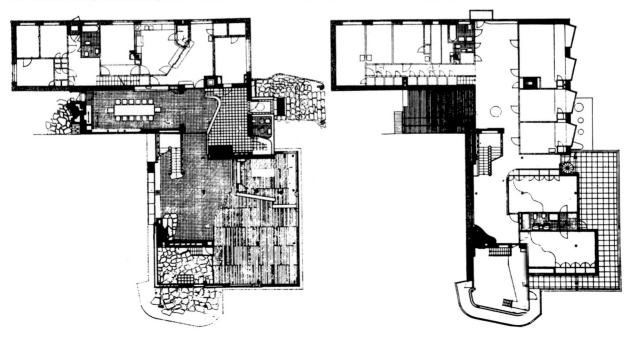

28. Villa Mairea. Entrance.

29. Villa Mairea. Exterior.

30. Villa Mairea. Exterior detail.

31. Villa Mairea. View of sauna, loggia, and pool.

32. Villa Mairea. Interior, corner of living room.

33. Sunila, 1936–39; 1951–54. View from harbor.

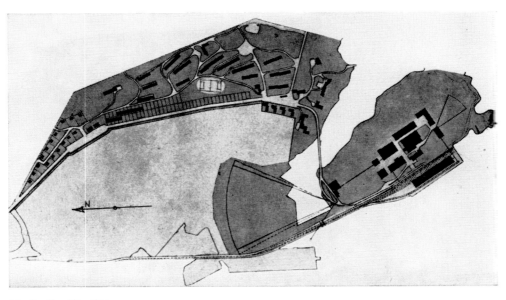

34. Sunila. Site plan.

35. Sunila. Sulphate Mill.

36. Sunila. Mill showing granite base.

37. Sunila. Sulphate Mill exterior.

38. Sunila. Sulphate Mill exterior.

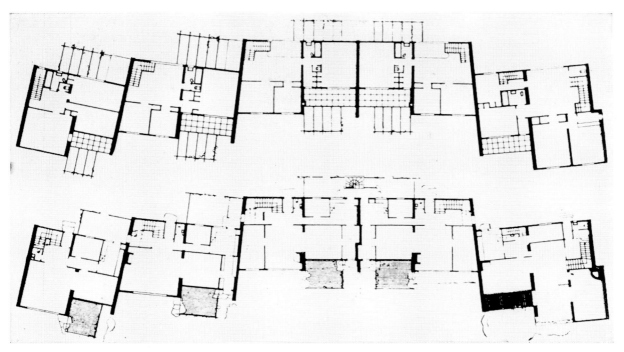

39. Sunila. Plan of engineers' housing.

40. Sunila. Worker's housing.

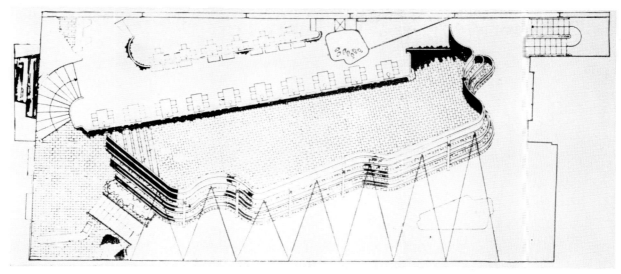

41. Finnish Pavilion. 1938–39. Plan.

42. Finnish Pavilion, New York World's Fair, 1938–39. Interior.

43. Stacking stools, 1938.

44. Upholstered chair with laminated spring arms, 1929–30.

45. Side chairs: low back with padded seat (left); high back with plywood seat (right).

46. Baker House Dormitory, Cambridge, Massachusetts, 1947–48. Exterior.

47. Baker House Dormitory. Plans of main floor (above) and typical floor (below).

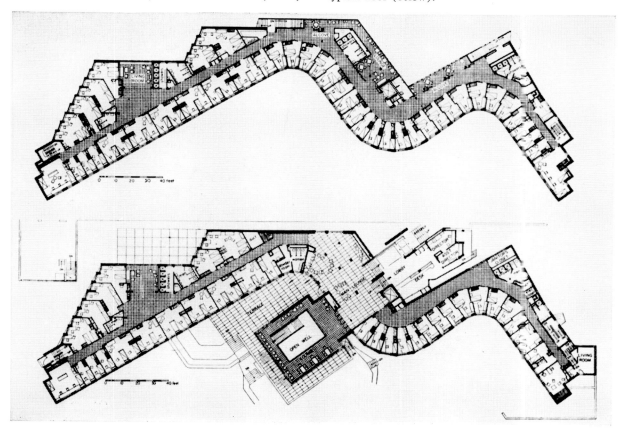

48. Baker House Dormitory. Exterior, street front.

49. Baker House Dormitory. Exterior, side wall.

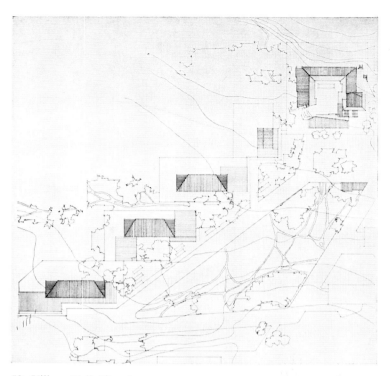

50. Village Hall. Site plan.

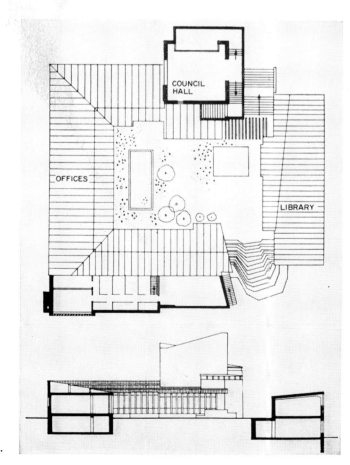

51. Village Hall. Plan (above), section (below).

52. Village Hall, Säynatsälo, 1950–51. Exterior.

53. Village Hall. Exterior.

54. Village Hall. Exterior, garden terrace wall.

55. Village Hall. Exterior.

56. Village Hall. Shops under library.

57. Village Hall. Exterior.

58. Village Hall. Interior court.

59. Village Hall. Council Chamber.

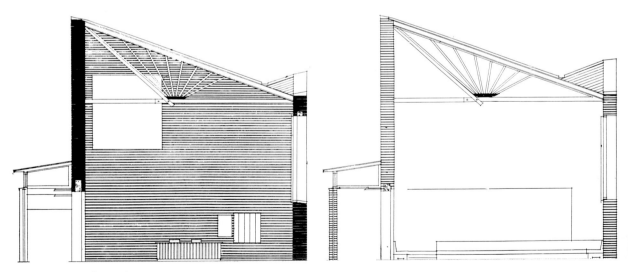

60. Village Hall. Sections.

61. Village Hall. Roof truss detail.

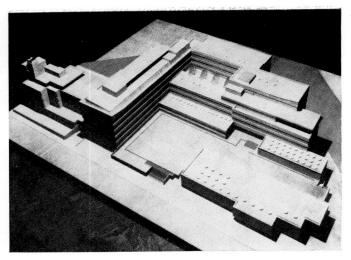

62. Pension Bank. Model, view from
    south.

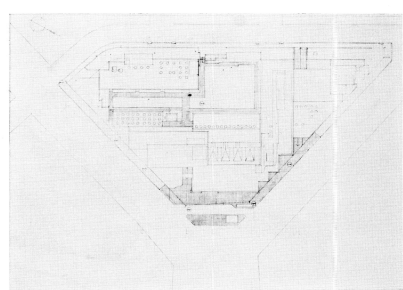

63. Pension Bank.
    Site and building plan.

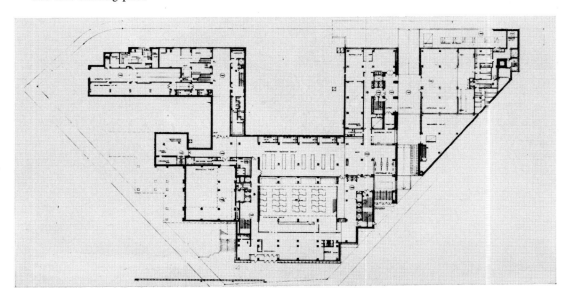

64. Pension Bank, Helsinki, 1952–56. Exterior from south.

65. Pension Bank. Exterior from south.

66. Pension Bank. Exterior and garden court.

67. Pension Bank. Exterior.

68. Pension Bank. Exterior.

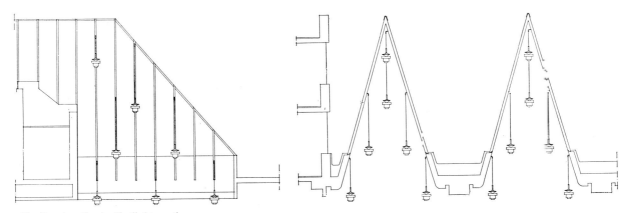

69. Pension Bank. Skylight section.

70. Pension Bank. Skylight.

71. Pension Bank. Skylight.

72. Pension Bank. Exterior, south elevation.

73. Pension Bank. Entrance.

74. Pension Bank. Facade detail.

75. Pension Bank. Employee cafeteria.

76. Pension Bank. Seminar-Reading room.

77. Pension Bank. Board Room.

78. Pension Bank. Committee meeting room.

79. Pension Bank. Offices.

80. Pension Bank. Lighting fixture.

81. Pension Bank. Lighting fixture.

82. Pension Bank. Lighting fixture.

83. Pension Bank. Lighting fixture.

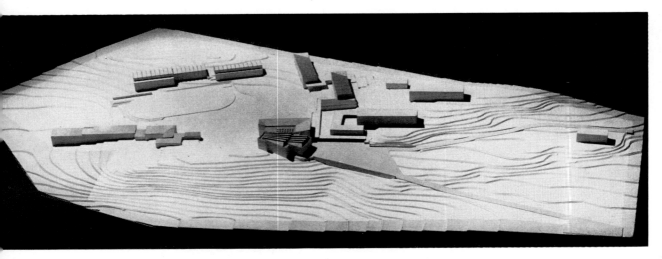

84. University, Jyväskylä, 1952–57. Site model.

85. University. Plan of administration building.

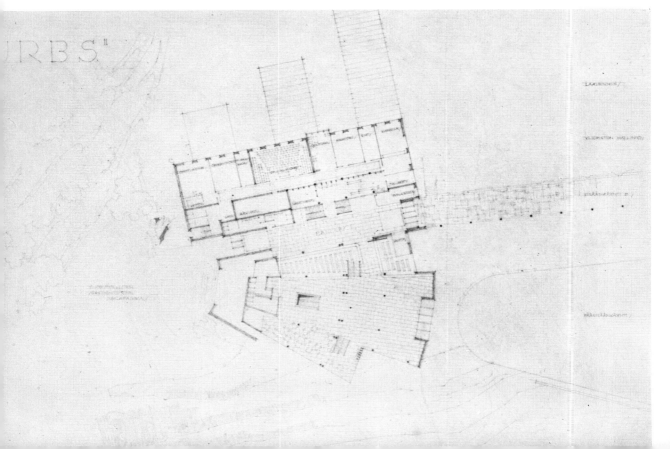

86. University. Exterior.

87. University. Exterior.

88. University. Students' dining room (temporary lighting fixtures).

89. University. Interior, staircase.

90. University. Main vestibule.

91. House of Culture, Helsinki, 1955–58. Exterior.

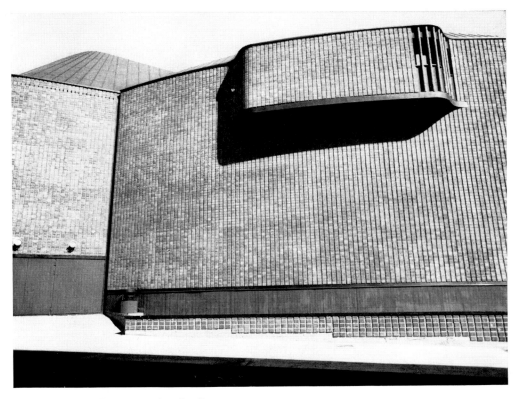

92. House of Culture. Exterior detail.

93. House of Culture. Entrance to Cinema.

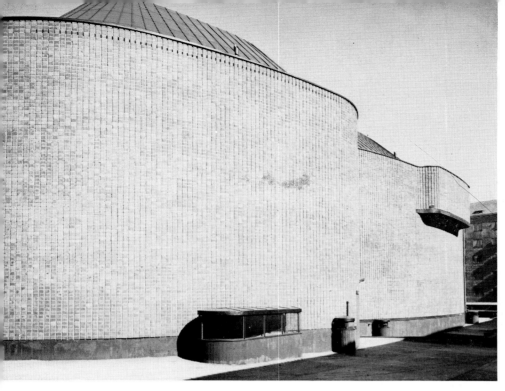

94. House of Culture. Entrance to Concert Hall.

95. House of Culture. Plan.

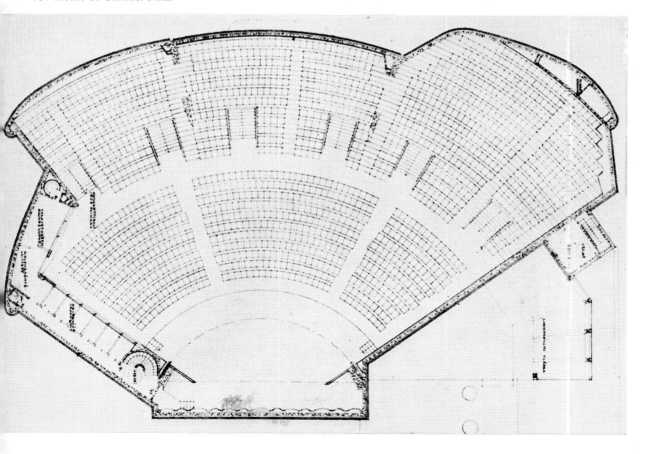

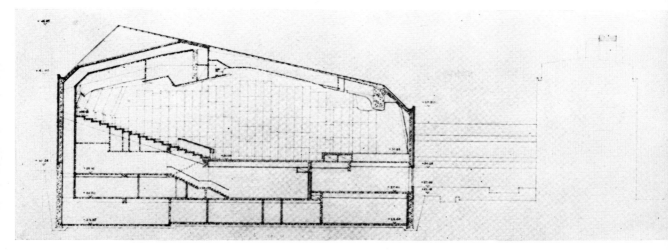

96. House of Culture. Section.

97. House of Culture. Concert Hall, interior.

98, 99, 100 & 101. House of Culture. Concert Hall, interior details.

102. Church, Vuoksenniska, 1956–58. Exterior.

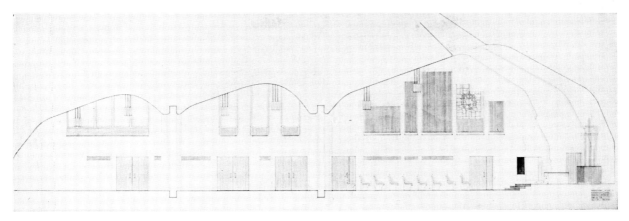

103. Church. Section.

104. Church. Exterior, showing storm-damaged site.

105. Church. Exterior detail.

106. Church. Exterior detail.

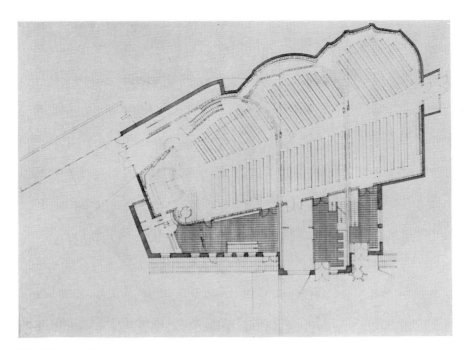

107. Church. Plan.

108. Church. Exterior.

109. Church. Interior.

110. Church. Interior (opposite page).

111. Church. Interior toward rear.

112. Church. Entrance lobby with skylight.

113. Church. Interior, window.

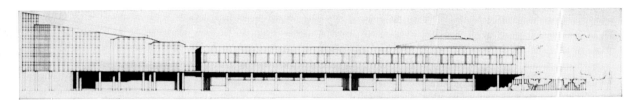

114. Cultural Center, Wolfsburg, Germany (under construction). Front elevation.

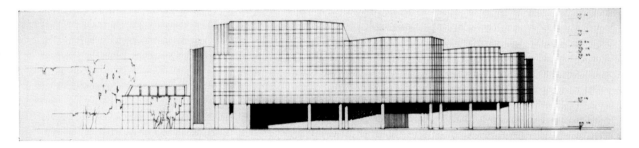

115. Cultural Center. Side elevation.

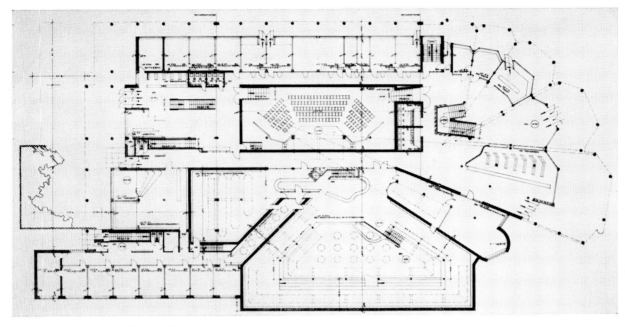

116. Cultural Center. Upper floor plan.

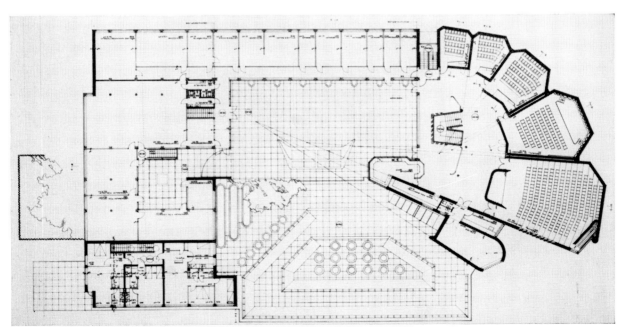

117. Cultural Center. Ground floor plan.

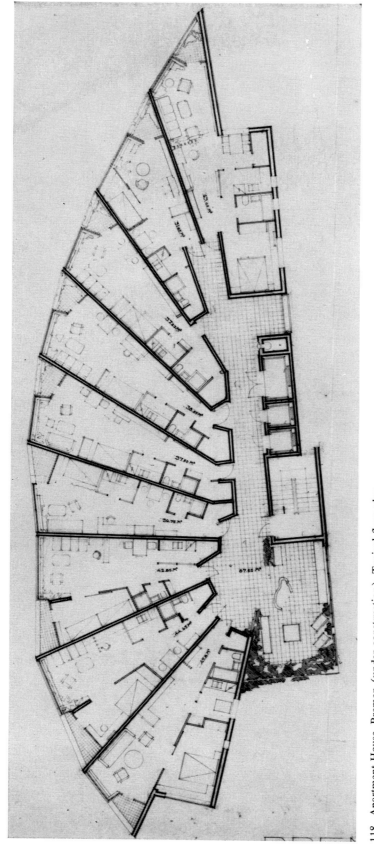

118. Apartment House, Bremen (under construction). Typical floor plan.

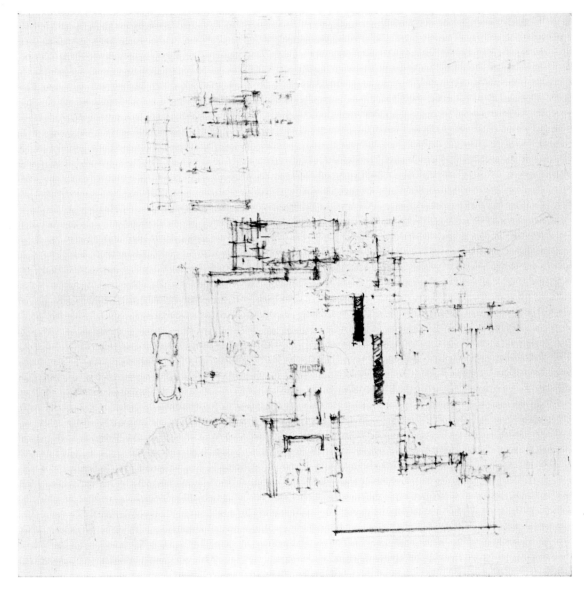

119. House for Mr. Louis Carré, Bazoches, France (under construction). Ground floor plan. Sketch by Aalto.

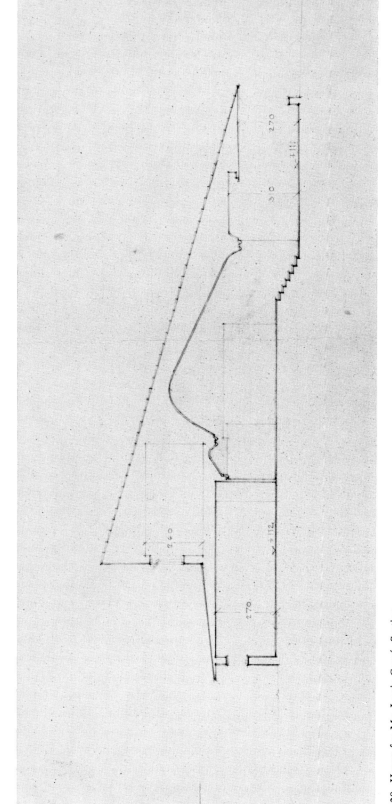

120. House for Mr. Louis Carré. Section.

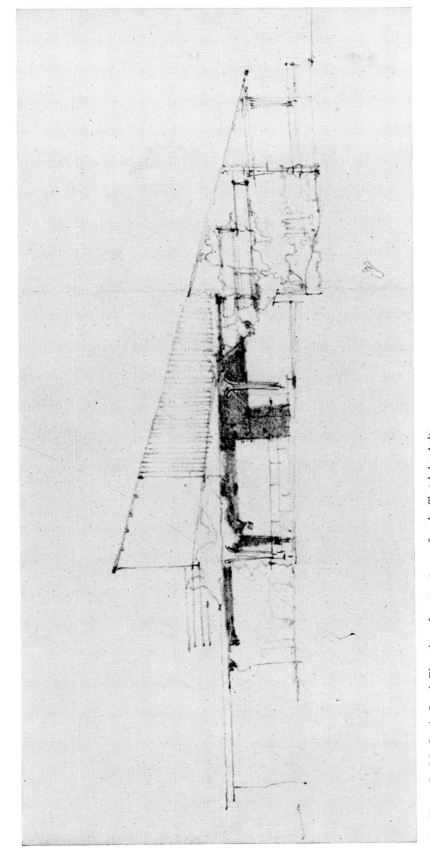

121. House for Mr. Louis Carré. Elevation of west entrance facade. Sketch by Aalto.

122. Art Center, Aalborg, Denmark (under construction). Model.

A NOTE ON TOURISM AND
ARCHITECTURE IN FINLAND

CHANGING TRAVEL habits as well as the airplane have brought Finland within the range of many European visitors. Since architecture can be fully understood only by looking at the buildings themselves, many readers of this book may reasonably plan to visit Finland. This note will provide some practical information and a few words about architecture in Finland beyond the works of Alvar Aalto.

The usual point of entry to Finland is at Helsinki or Turku. Although the journey via Finland's national airline, Finnair, is little more than an hour from Stockholm, the highly recommended overnight steamer from Stockholm is comfortable, clean and pleasant, with excellent meals and a memorable early arrival at Turku, through the Åland archipelago. The boat directly to Helsinki takes a few hours longer, but the arrival by water again provides an unforgettable sight of the capital's monumental buildings, as well as an invaluable key to the "white city" and its principal features. Finland can also be reached directly from many other ports, including New York City.

Within Finland travel is easy and relatively cheap via Finnair's domestic service or the many bus lines. Travel by private car is also recommended, although rather high Baltic ferry charges and the limited mileage of hard-surfaced roads make it advisable to consider renting a car in Finland unless a long trip is planned. Travel by car is unquestionably the best way to make the most of a limited amount of time, facilitating visits to outlying areas. The points of architectural interest are quite widely scattered. Language difficulties cannot be minimized, but are seldom insurmountable.

The high tourist season of July and August offers the most pleasant weather, but presents the usual obstacle of crowded accommodations. The very pleasant and convenient lake steamers operate during the summer months only. June and September are better months on the whole, if the traveller can choose. The early fall colors are superb.

The standard English language guide is *Finland* (1953) in the Nagel Travel Guide Series. Among several national highway maps, that issued by Shell is especially good. Finnish national tourist offices, consulates, and travel agents can provide abundant free literature and maps. In Helsinki and other principal cities municipal tourist information offices are maintained. One excellent and cheap photographic survey of the country is Matti Poutvaara's *Suomi-Finland* (Porvoo, 1958), which has many of the character-istics of a guidebook as well.

For other literature on the country and its people, the book department in Stock-mann's department store is especially recommended, and its foreign language section is the largest in the country. For older books and historical prints, visit Nordiska Bokhandel, Fabiansgatan 17, situated in a district containing other antiquarian shops.

The architectural visitor should communicate with Finland's Architecture Museum, Parkgatan 4, Helsinki, whose director is the art historian Kyosti Ålander. This institu-tion is open from 10 A.M to 3 P.M. The Museum offers periodic exhibitions, compre-hensive information on all aspects of Finnish architecture including photographs, and will assist in organizing visits to the principal buildings of architectural interest. Through the Museum it may be possible to plan all or part of one's visit to advantage with others sharing the same interest.

The Architecture Museum is supported in part by the Finnish Architectural Society, whose headquarters are at Ainogatan 3, Helsinki. The Society also publishes the monthly illustrated professional journal *Arkkitehti-Arkitekten.*

Probably the best itinerary for a comprehensive tour would be based on Helsinki, the center from which radiate the principal communications to all parts of the nation. The capital city contains most, but by no means all, of the principal architectural masterpieces, and provides a good orientation to the national architecture as a whole. From here a series of circular journeys can be planned. One such trip might embrace Turku, including the Paimio sanatorium, Pori and other places of interest in south-western Finland. A second could include Lahti, the unique Gothic church at Hattula and the Aulanko park, Tampere and other cities immediately north of Helsinki. A third could include the old Baltic port cities like Porvoo, the industrial port of Kotka and the wood products centers of southeastern Finland; and by a further extension of this trip, a visit to the oustandingly beautiful and historic fortress at Olavinlinna.

Longer journeys can be made to Jyväskylä, and to such urban centers of northern Finland as the Baltic port of Oulu, or Rovaniemi, the "capital" of Lapland. Such extended trips, due to the considerable distances involved, are probably best made by air.

In Helsinki a brief list of important buildings would embrace the neo-classic monu-ments, principally by the architect C. L. Engel, the City Hall, the University library and related buildings, and the Senate Square including the cathedral; Eliel Saarinen's railroad station; Frosterus' Stockmann's department store; J. S. Siren's Parliament House; and Yrjo Lindegren's Olympic stadium.

Of the buildings by Alvar Aalto, the ones whose interiors may be conveniently visited are the Iron House and Artek Store, the Savoy Restaurant, the House of Culture (during hours of performances), and the Pension Bank (by arrangement with the appropriate official who in 1958 was Mr. Lippaner).

Among other important modern buildings in Helsinki that might be seen are Vilja Rewell's Palace Hotel; Aarne Ervi's University Institute and the Marine Terminal; Kaija and Heikki Siren's addition to the National Theatre; and the new garden city of Tapiola, six miles west of the city, containing the work of a number of excellent younger architects. In addition to the three architects named, the great contemporaries in Finland include Jorma Jarvi, Markus Tavio, Jonas Cedarcreutz, and Keijo Petaja. In the embassy quarter of the city is found an enormous neo-classic Soviet embassy, constructed by the Finns as a part of their reparations payment; and there will be shortly a new addition to the United States embassy designed by Harwell Hamilton Harris.

In general, it may be said that visits to the interiors of buildings are always more satisfactory if arranged in advance so that someone can show them properly. Churches in Finland, for example, are ordinarily closed except during services. Only a small part of hospitals or schools are ordinarily open to the public. An added dimension of appreciation of a theatre or a concert hall is provided by visiting it during a performance.

The city of Helsinki itself—whose inhabitants constitute some ten percent of the national population of 4,000,000—deserves mention for its general plan. The view from the water is especially pleasant, but failing this it may be very well appreciated from the terrace of the Marine Terminal. There are several high points of vantage, including the top of the tower of the stadium and the roof of the Torni Hotel. The Market Square, Station Square, Esplanade and the principal parks are key features of the city. The city publishes an excellent tourist map with information concerning public transportation. While out of print, an architectural guide to Helsinki (1955) prepared by the Architectural Society for use with this map is being revised.

CHRONOLOGY

1898	Born Hugo Alvar Henrik Aalto, February 3, in parish of Kuortana, in West Central Finland.
	Educated in local schools, and Technical High School, Helsinki.
1919	Military service during War of National Liberation.
1921	Graduated in architecture.
1921–23	Travel in Sweden and Europe.
1923–27	Established architectural office, Jyväskylä.
1925	Marriage to and beginning of collaboration with Aino Marsio (1898?–1949). All professional work in this period is the result of this collaboration.
1927–33	Office in Turku. Association with Erik Bryggman.
1928	Member, Congrés International d'Architecture Moderne.
1931	Lectures in Norway.
1932	First chair designs.
1933–	Office in Helsinki; later in Munkkiniemi, a suburb.
1933	Exhibitions in London, Zurich.
1935	Artek Ltd. founded for manufacture and distribution of furniture.
1936	Commenced service as architect for Ahlstrom Company.
1938	First visit to United States, exhibition in Museum of Modern Art.
1939	Service in ski battalion during 'winter war" with U.S.S.R.
1940	Appointed professor, College of Architecture, Massachusetts Institute of Technology.
1947	Awarded honorary degree of Doctor of Fine Arts, Princeton University.
1952	Marriage to Elissa Makiniemi.
1954	Exhibition at Zurich.
1955	Member, Finnish Academy.
1957	Awarded Gold Medal, Royal Institute of British Architects.

A CHRONOLOGICAL LIST OF BUILDINGS

AND SELECTED PROJECTS (1922–1958)

1922	Industrial Exhibit	Tampere
1923–25	Labor Party Headquarters Theatre	Jyväskylä
1924	Church remodelling	Äänekosken
1924	Church remodelling	Anttolan
1926	Church remodelling	Tampere
1927–28	Theatre	Turku
1927–29	Church	Muurame
1927–35	Municipal library	Viipuri
1929	Church remodelling	Kemijärvi
1928	Apartments	Turku
1929	700th Anniversary Exhibition	Turku
	(with Erik Bryggman)	Turku
1923–30	Offices of Turun-Sanomat Newspaper	Paimio
1929–33	Tuberculosis Sanatorium	Toppila
1930–31	Sulphate Paper mill	Tampere
1934	Railroad Station	Tallin (Esthonia)
1934	Art Museum	Munkkiniemi
1934	Apartments	Munkkiniemi
1935–36	Architect's own house	
1936–39; 1951–54	Sulphate pulp mill and housing	Sunila
1937	Finland pavilion, Paris Exposition	Paris
1937	Savoy restaurant	Helsinki
1938	Pavilion in agricultural fair	Lapua
1938–39	Finland pavilion interior, New York World's Fair	New York
1938–39	Villa Mairea, House for Mr. and Mrs. Harry Gullichson	Noormarku
1938–39	Paper factory	Inkeroinen
1938–39	Multiple housing	Kauttua
1939–45	Employees housing	Karhula

1942–46	Town plan	Säynätsalo
1944–45	Town plan (with Lindegren, Saarnio, Tavio and Simberg)	Rovaniemi
1944	Town center plan (with Albin Stark)	Avesta
1944–47	Apartments	Vaasa
1945	Sawmill	Varkaus
1945	Town center plan	Oulu
1946	Sauna at Villa Mairea	Noormarku
1946	Town plan	Nynäshaimin
1946	Exhibition pavilion	Hedemora
1947	Regional plan and town center plan	Imatra
1947	Johnson Institute (Project)	Avesta
1947–48	Baker House, Massachusetts Institute of Technology	Cambridge, Mass. (U.S.A.)
1949–55	Master plan, Technical Institute	Otaniemi
1949	Storage warehouse	Karhula
1950	Burial grounds (Project)	Malmi
1950–51	Village hall	Säynätsalo
1951	Entrance pavilion, Skillnaden	Helsinki
1951	Nitrogen works site plan	Oulu
1951	Theatre (Project)	Kuopio
1951	Enso-Gutzeit plant	Kotka
1952	Enso-Gutzeit country club	Kallvik
1952–56	National Pensions Institute	Helsinki
1952–57	Pedagogic University of Jyväskylä master plan and principal buildings	Jyväskylä
1952–58	Church	Seinäjoki
1952–54	Sports hall	Otaniemi
1952	Engineers club and restaurant	Helsinki
1952–54	Iron House, office building	Helsinki
1952–54	Housing for employees, National Pensions Institute	Helsinki
1953	Architect's own summer house	Muuratsalo
1953	Enso-Gutzeit plant	Summa
1953	Lyngby Crematorium and chapel (Project)	Copenhagen
1953	Sports Hall (Project)	Vienna
1955	Technical college (Project)	Oulu
1955	Theatre and Concert Hall (Project)	Oulu
1955–58	House of Culture	Helsinki
1955–57	Apartments in building exhibition	Berlin
1955	Studio House (architect's own office)	Munkkiniemi
1955	Town Hall (Project)	Gothenburg (Sweden)
1956	Finland pavilion, Bienniale	Venice
1956	Port facility (Project)	Gothenburg (Sweden)
1956–59	House for Louis Carré	Bazoches (France)
1956–58	Church	Vuoksenniska

1957	University Master plan	Oulu
1958	Art Museum (Project)	Bagdad
1958	Post and Telegraph Office	Bagdad
1958	Cultural Center	Wolfsburg (Germany)
1958	Apartments	Bremen
1958	Town hall (Project)	Kiruna
1958	Art Center	Aalborg (Denmark)
1958	Housing community	Rovaniemi

SELECTED BIBLIOGRAPHY

Aalto, Alvar, *Post-War Reconstruction. Rehousing Research in Finland.* (New York, 1941?) Privately printed to aid the Finnish reconstruction movement, this contains a valuable exposition of Aalto's planning and housing ideas.

Aalto, Alvar, "Zwischen Humanismus und Materialismus," *Baukunst und Werkform,* No. 6, 1956. pp. 298–300.

"Alvar Aalto, Architecture and Furniture," catalog of exhibition, 1939, at the Museum of Modern Art, New York City. The first work of significance on Aalto to appear in the United States, this volume containing an essay by Simon Breines on architecture and one by A. Lawrence Kocher on furniture, still contains much of interest.

"Alvar Aalto in the Finnish Forests: Civic Center for Säynätsalo," *Architectural Forum,* April, 1954, pp. 148–153.

"Alvar und Aino Aalto," catalog of exhibition, June, 1948, at the Kunstgewerbemuseum, Zurich, Wegleitung 175. The introductory text by Siegfried Giedion, as well as nearly all the illustrations, duplicate the material in the 1949 edition of *Space, Time and Architecture.* (See Giedion, Siegfried.)

"Alvar Aalto," *Zodiac #3,* Milan, 1958. Issue devoted primarily to illustrations of Aalto's later work with essays by Pier Carlo Santini and Göran Schildt.

Architecture in Finland, Helsinki, 1932. A compendium published by Finland's National Architectural Society.

Arkkitehti-Arkitekten, January–February, 1958. Special double issue of the magazine devoted entirely to the Pension Bank and an extensive review of Aalto's life work on the occasion of his 60th birthday.

Banham, R., "One and the Few. The Rise of Modern Architecture in Finland," *Architectural Review,* April, 1957, pp. 243–251; 256–257. An excellent survey which examines especially the position of Aalto among his younger contemporaries and immediate predecessors.

Burchard, John, "Finland and Architect Aalto," *Architectural Record,* January, 1959, pp. 125–136. A summary estimate of Aalto's position in architecture today by a former academic associate at the Massachusetts Institute of Technology.

"Contemporary Finnish Architecture," catalog of exhibition at the Octagon, headquarters of the American Institute of Architects, circulated by the Smithsonian Institute, Washington, 1955. The catalog contains a foreword by Alvar Aalto. It also stimulated the publication in the *Architectural Record,* February, 1956, pp. 161–168 of an excellent appreciation by Göran Schildt.

Giedion, Siegfried, *Space, Time and Architecture,* Cambridge, 1949. The eighth printing of this classic interpretation of modern architecture, first issued in 1941, added at pp. 453–492 an entire chapter on Alvar Aalto which remains the best critical treatment of the architect's work.

Giedion, Siegfried, "Alvar Aalto," *Architectural Review,* February, 1950, pp. 77–84.

Goldstone, Harman, "Alvar Aalto," *American Magazine of Art,* April, 1939. Vol. 32, pp. 208 ff.

Gutheim, Frederick, "Free Finland, the New Chapter," *Survey Graphic,* April, 1941.

Kidder-Smith, G. E., "Alvar Aalto," *American Scandinavian Review,* December, 1940. Vol. 28, pp. 313–320.

Labo, Georgia, *Alvar Aalto,* (Il Balcone Series) Milan, 1948.

"M.I.T. Senior Dormitory," *Architectural Forum,* August, 1949, pp. 61–69. (Now called Baker House).

Neuenschwander, Ed. and Cl., *Finnish Architecture and Alvar Aalto,* New York, 1954. Aalto through the eyes of two Swiss students who worked in his office. The flashes of insight into Aalto's work encountered in the writing of Giedion and a few other critics seem like a distant lightning in a wide landscape when contrasted with the poetic closeup given by the Neuenschwanders. While they see the Finns through rose-tinted glasses, the poetry of their writing and the imagery of their photographic montage cannot be denied. They concentrate on the projects with which they became most familiar while working in Aalto's office during the early 1950's, but to these are added discriminating insights into earlier work. One third of the entire book is an introduction of Finland's geography, people and culture.

Paulsson, Thomas, *Scandinavian Architecture,* London, 1959. An excellent introduction of deep historical penetration which, unlike most surveys of its sort, does not distort the position of Finland.

Roth, Alfred, *The New Architecture,* Zurich, 1940. Contains at pp. 181–194 the best description of the Viipuri library.

Sears, H., "A Visit to Säynätsalo," *Royal Architectural Institute of Canada Journal,* September, 1957, pp. 340–342.

Waris, Heikki, *Social Institutions in Finland.* University of Helsinki, Institute of Social Policy, Reprint Series B, No. 1 (University of Minnesota Press, Minneapolis, Minn. 1958). A convenient and up-to-date work, giving the main sociological, economic and political facts about Finland.

The architectural magazines of the world have dealt extensively with individual buildings designed by Alvar Aalto. Those of particular importance might include the journal of the Finnish Architectural Society, Arkkitehti-Arkitekten; L'Architecture d'Aujourd'hui; Werk; the Architectural Review, London; Architectural Forum; Architectural Record; and Progressive Architecture. Additional material will be found in the various exhibitions on Finnish architecture, prepared for foreign showing by the Finnish Architectural Society and the Finnish Architectural Museum. Fugitive material of some value, frequently with illustrations, has been published on most of the important buildings such as the Paimio Sanatorium, and the Pension Bank. The Ahlstrom Company and Artek have also issued publications of specialized value.

SOURCES OF ILLUSTRATIONS

Albin Aaltonen, Jyväskylä: 86, 88

Architect's Journal; Sept. 10, 1946: 10

Architectural Record; Jan., 1959: 51

Artek, Helsinki: 32

Jane Doggett, New York: 79, 91, 92, 93, 94, 99, 100, 101, 105, 106, 109, 110

Frederick Gutheim, Washington, D. C.: 26, 28, 29, 30, 55, 56, 57, 72, 74, 78, 103, 108, 111, 112

Heikki Havas, Helsinki: 33, 35, 36, 38, 64, 65, 66, 67, 68, 70, 71, 73, 75, 76, 77, 82, 83, 89, 90, 97, 98, 102, 113, 122

G. E. Kidder-Smith, New York: 37

Courtesy Massachusetts Institute of Technology, Cambridge, Massachusetts: 46, 48, 49

Courtesy Museum of Modern Art, New York: 1, 2, 3, 4, 5, 6, 7, 8, 9, 12, 13, 15, 16, 17, 22, 23, 24, 25, 27, 41, 43, 44, 45

Neuenschwander E. & C., *Finnish Architecture and Alvar Aalto* (New York, 1954): 50, 60

Courtesy Smithsonian Institute, Washington, D. C.: 20, 53, 54

Ezra Stoller, Rye, New York: 42

Valokuva, Kolmio: 58, 59, 87

Werk; Oct., 1934: 18, 19, 21; Mar./Apr., 1940: 11, 34; Apr., 1950: 47

Zodiac #3, 1958: 95, 96

INDEX

Numbers in regular roman type refer to text pages; *italic* figures refer to the plates.